THE WESTERN HIGHLANDS

1 (overleaf) Loch Hope and Ben Hope in Sutherland: classic deer forest and salmon fishing in lonely country

TOM WEIR

Photographs by the Author

THE WESTERN HIGHLANDS

B. T. Batsford Ltd
London

©Tom Weir 1973
First published 1973
Second impression 1976

ISBN 0 7134 0079 X

Printed in Great Britain by Biddles Ltd, Guildford, Surrey,
for the publishers B. T. Batsford Ltd, 4 Fitzhardinge Street,
London W1H 0AH

CONTENTS

THE ILLUSTRATIONS

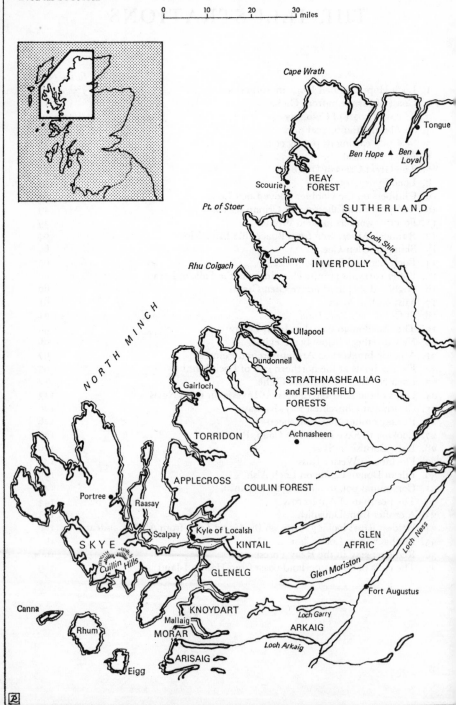

THE WESTERN HIGHLANDS

North section

0   10   20   30 miles

Cape Wrath

Tongue

Ben Hope ▲   Ben ▲
                Loyal

Scourie

REAY
FOREST

SUTHERLAND

Pt. of Stoer

Loch Shin

Rhu Coigach

Lochinver

INVERPOLLY

NORTH MINCH

Ullapool

Dundonnell

STRATHNASHEALLAG
and FISHERFIELD
FORESTS

Gairloch

TORRIDON

Achnasheen

APPLECROSS

COULIN FOREST

Portree

Raasay

GLEN
AFFRIC

Loch Ness

Scalpay

Kyle of Localsh

KINTAIL

SKYE

Cuillin Hills

GLENELG

Glen Moriston

Fort Augustus

Canna

KNOYDART

Mallaig

MORAR

Loch Garry

ARKAIG

Rhum

ARISAIG

Loch Arkaig

Eigg

THE WESTERN HIGHLANDS

South section

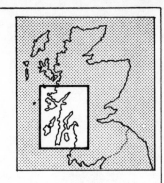

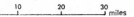

10   20   30 miles

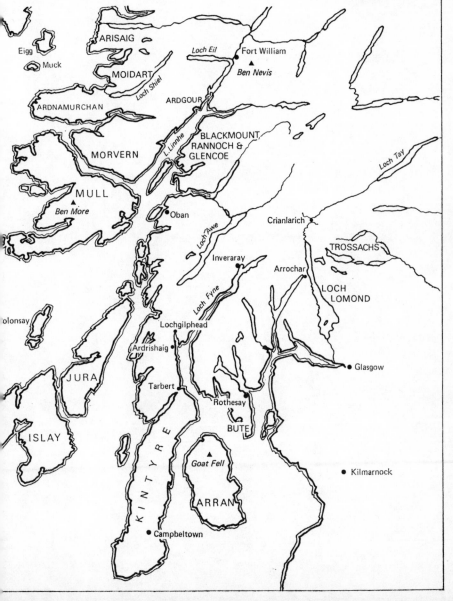

Eigg

Muck

ARISAIG

MOIDART

Loch Eil   Fort William

Ben Nevis ▲

Loch Shiel

ARDNAMURCHAN   ARDGOUR

MORVERN   *L. Linnhe*   BLACKMOUNT RANNOCH & GLENCOE

Loch Tay

MULL ▲

Ben More   •Oban

Loch Awe   Crianlarich

TROSSACHS

Inveraray   Arrochar

LOCH LOMOND

Loch Fyne

olonsay

Lochgilphead

Ardrishaig •   •Glasgow

JURA   Tarbert

Rothesay

BUTE

ISLAY   K I N T Y R E   *Goat Fell* ▲

• Kilmarnock

ARRAN

•Campbeltown

Introduction

The more you know of a subject, the more you respect it. If you understand sand dunes, and the way they are held together by specially adapted grasses and plants of the seashore, you are unlikely to drive your motor car randomly onto the beach, and so cause destruction by erosion. If you are thrilled by the primeval forest of Caledonian pines, whose roots go back into prehistory, you will not light a fire against the bark of one of these unique trees, leaving it charred and damaged, hall-marked by vandalism.

Yet we cannot expect tourists to be well-informed, especially in the far west of Scotland which seems so vast and remote, where the narrow roads swing in and out of inviting bays, where clear streams run through rock pavements bearing ice-age plants, and unusual birds nest on the shore, or on cliff ledges yellow with roseroot or bright with seapinks.

In pre-motor car days few travelled this far country, and even as late as the mid-'30s not many working people had time or money enough to explore in regions not only badly served by roads, but run down to the point of economic failure. The Western Highlands were virtually sporting estates, employing a few ghillies, keepers, house servants and handymen. Crofters lived at mere subsistence level. Inshore fisheries had been spoiled by illegal trawling, so it was hardly surprising that the main export of the region was men and women, bound for Australia, Canada, Glasgow or London.

You do not have to proclaim any political faith to state that this *laissez faire* situation was no use to Scotland or Britain as a whole. It took the course of the Second World War to reverse this period of indifference to the principles of wise land use. But first of all we had to pay the price. For failing to grow enough commercial timber for our needs, we had to hack down priceless remnants of primeval forest. By not developing hydro-electricity we found ourselves short of vital power for our factories. Suddenly we valued our farmers, and began to enrich the land which is the true life-blood of an island race.

North and north-western Scotland was declared a restricted area in the war. Why? Because the deep sea lochs sheltered by mountains were being used as assembly points for great convoys of ships. The Navy experimented here with magnetic mines, while Commando troops trained for destruction tasks on sea-cliffs and hills, destroying unfortunately a vast acreage of Caledonian wood on Loch Arkaigside when it caught alight during an exercise.

Luckily the dynamism of war was carried into the peace, with a vast programme of tree planting by the Forestry Commission, the building of dams and power houses by the North of Scotland Hydro-electric Board; the establishment of an Atomic Reactor at Dounreay on the Pentland Firth, while in Fort William an integrated pulp mill was built, to marry timber and water and produce high-grade paper products.

Fort William offers factory workers an alternative to city life. True there is the acrid smell of industry and the urbanism of new housing schemes, and ugly pipes sprouting out of Ben Nevis carrying water from Loch Treig through the mountain to power the British Aluminium factory. Nearby Kinlochleven has been called the ugliest township on the 2,000 miles of coast covered by this book, but it too is an aluminium town, providing jobs for a thousand in a Norwegian-type setting at the head of a fjord.

But the major industry in the Western Highlands since the end of the war has been tourism. Prosperity in terms of shorter hours of work, higher pay, longer holidays and universal car-ownership meant that the Western Highlands lay within easy driving distance of any British centre. Climbers and skiers from London, Birmingham, Sheffield, Durham and elsewhere began arriving in Glen Coe every weekend. The joys of our cold snowy winters had been discovered.

In summer, campers by the thousand found their Atlantic paradise, and soon empty houses were being snatched up as holiday homes. The 'Highland Season' now belongs to us all, and inevitably there are problems of litter, trespass, conflict with sporting interest and amenity problems, due to failure to cope with the sheer volume of the invasion.

All this is a far cry from the unemployment of the '30s and the days of the cyclist who was the spearhead of the outdoor revolution before the new cult of 'hiking' suddenly became popular. There was peace on the roads then, when Clydesdale horses by the hundred still clip-clopped the cobbled streets of Glasgow. True there was bitter political feeling, but never before in the history of Scotland had so many people turned to their native countryside for inspiration in a drab world.

Summer and winter down the twenty miles of the west shore of Loch Lomond you would see the red blaze of cyclists' fires, dozens of them, each with a ring of young faces round it. Get close and you would see black tea-cans perched on the fire rim—usually home-made from a syrup tin and a piece of wire for handle—and at the cry of 'man-up', a handful of tea would be thrown into the bubbling water, and its owner would withdraw to add sugar and drink the brew straight from the can.

No cups, and no litter either, for these hard-pushing cyclists travelled light, with little more than sandwiches and a cape in their saddle-bags. These men took pride in packing gear for a whole weekend into tiny space in the pre-plastic age. The era of the motor-car boot full of disposable rubbish was yet to come. But they covered as much ground as most motorists, getting as far away as Kintail from Glasgow in a long weekend.

I was one of that first generation of outdoor folk. Newly out of school and with a passion for natural history and mountains, my ambition was to live in the Western Highlands, and become a shepherd, or a keeper. Alas, the prospects were not encouraging. Prices for wool and mutton were so low that hirsels could hardly pay shepherds' wages. Deer forests were going unlet, and there was little more than seasonal work to be had, ghillieing or repairing paths.

Super-tax and the depression had ended the dream days of deer forest ownership which had lasted the best part of ninety years by the time I arrived on the scene. Most of the wealthy aristocrats and industrialists who had built the shooting lodges had died or were considerably poorer. The peak period was 1912 when 203 deer forests occupied 3.5 million acres. They still account for 2,800,000 acres today.

The reader of this book will discover my own attitude to the deer forest. In my early days as a climber I revelled in the great uninhabited wildernesses among the glens and long sea lochs of the Western Highlands. For me it was akin to being an explorer of an empty land which I took as natural. I had not the perception then to realize that I was looking upon a landscape devastated by overgrazing by sheep and deer, whose woodlands had been as effectively cleared as its people. Ancient history to me became modern as I opened the book of knowledge and realized that this run-down of land, and the eviction of those who lived on it, dated only from the eighteenth century. I began to re-explore the Western Highlands anew, and this is what this book is about. It is a reappraisal, after forty years' wandering, and it comes as the whole North is on the brink of its first industrial revolution with the discovery of oil under the seabed.

At this stage it is impossible to assess the impact of oil and its related industries. But just as the pulp mill and the aluminium works at Fort William and Kinlochleven are staffed mainly by incomers, it seems likely that the same will happen with oil. Yet this is no argument against development, if the correct planning decisions are made and the strictest controls imposed safeguarding the environment. But the enemy of this good planning is speed. Haste should be made slowly here, and no high amenity site should be abused until it has been proved that nothing lesser will do.

After all, look at the time scale of man in the Western Highlands. Compared to the clock-face of history, the Azilians did not arrive on our shores until a few seconds before midnight. Stone-age man was roaming Africa 60,000 years ago when ice-sheets so covered the Western Highlands that they stretched far beyond the Outer Hebrides. These moving ice-sheets waxed and waned, to a last major advance that occurred between 25,000 and 10,000 years ago.

Originally Scotland had been a high plateau heaved up from the flat by a buckling earth-movement. The forces of erosion working over 30 million years had moulded valleys and hollows when the build-up of ice began, its moving weight carving the plateau into the peaks and valleys we know today. When man arrived in his skin-boats on the west coast 7,000–9,000 years ago glaciers still choked the high corries, but everywhere else was forest or marsh. These are the people who left their stone and flint implements on Oronsay as described in Chapter One.

Theirs was a fringe existence, living on the shore in a climate

2 *Jura seen from the ice-scored rocks of Gigha*

3 *Colonsay: Beinn Bhreac plunges to the sea in cliffs where seabirds nest*

sometimes warmer than any we know today, and sometimes considerably colder. We know about these weather fluctuations from analysis of buried pollen grains, revealing to us changes of vegetation as dwarf birch and arctic willows were replaced by pine and birch, to be replaced in turn by wet-loving alder.

These Azilian people gathering shellfish and using bone and flint tools lived from day to day, like animals, eating what they could find. But in Mesopotamia and Egypt at this time civilization was far advanced. The people lived in villages, knew the art of cultivating crops, had tamed wild animals to domestic use, practised the skills of pottery, could write in the Cuneiform script, and apply mathematical science to architecture.

It was the successors of these Middle East people who were to change the face of Scotland, though it took several thousand years for them to work their way across Europe, spreading their culture before them. The Neolithic farmers colonized Southern England about 2500 BC, but they did not penetrate even Galloway until a considerable time later. Significantly, they arrived at a time of climatic optimum, when conditions were drier and warmer than any period since then.

These farmers, using the sea as their highway left megalithic burial tombs behind them, in Jutland, Holland, and on the Atlantic coast of Eire, Brittany, and along the Mediterranean to Cyprus, right back to Syria. But they were not yet masters of their environment, though at Skara Brae in Orkney we can see they were a well organized people by the quality of their stone-furnished homestead.

Then followed the 'Beaker Folk'—the round-headed people who ushered in the Bronze Age. Now, the Neolithic farmers could till the soil with hoes, and their implements of metal gave them a greater command over nature. The numerous standing stones and circles in western Scotland belong to this period, as do cup and ring markings on rocks, preceding the Iron Age which did not begin in Scotland until nearly 2,000 years ago.

The Iron-Age conquerors were Kelts, people akin to the ancient Galli—Bretons, Cornish, Welsh, Irish and Manx. They spoke Gaelic, and they knew how to make implements to clear the forest, drain the marshes, plough the land, rear cattle for milk and beef, herd sheep and cut its wool with shears for spinning and weaving into cloth.

4   *An Atlantic seal pup weighs 30 pounds at birth and cries like a baby*

5   *In two weeks the pup begins to cast its first coat*

6   *Adolescent at three weeks, the young Atlantic seal is abandoned forever by its mother*

It is with these well-armed people that we move into written history, for it was the Kelts who built hill-top forts as defence against the Romans who invaded Scotland in AD 83. And these were the people, or their descendants, who built the brochs, these enormous defence towers which speckle the landscape of Sutherland, the Hebrides, Skye, Orkney and Shetland. They are unique to Scotland.

Nature no longer ruled the landscape of Scotland as the Romans built their walls, cut down swathes of trees to lay roads, or prevent ambush. Fire became a weapon of war to burn out tribes as well as to extirpate animals. The Viking invasions of the eleventh century wreaked destruction of the forest on an unprecedented scale. And the period of its happening coincided with a worsening of climate, when trees unprotected by other trees were blown down, to be covered up in peat as on Rannoch Moor, where you may see the bleaching skeletons of Caledonian pines in the rocky hollows.

Much of the destruction of Rannoch and other woods was done to extirpate wolves and men sheltering in the deep forest. Wild life was in retreat. Red deer became lighter in weight and smaller in size. The wolf became extinct just before the '45. But long before that the northern lynx, the reindeer and the elk had disappeared, together with the beaver and the ox.

And with the failure of the '45 Rising the Highlands were opened to the developers, anxious to exploit the new reserves of timber for smelting iron. Furnaces known as 'bloomeries' were erected wherever there was a big enough supply of trees, nor did they stop working until the woods were spent. Coincident with this was the introduction of large-scale sheep farming, resulting in over-intensive grazing and eventually a creeping tide of bracken.

The industrial revolution, and cheaper ways of smelting iron with coal saved some remnants of the primeval forest from the furnace—a forest which had been regenerating naturally for something like 9,000 years—yet it was not valued, not even by the new rich who destroyed priceless timber to make sheep grazings and later convert the new pastures to deer forests when the sheep failed.

Game preservation was the thing now. Shooting and the agricultural revolution went together, and it is true that much of the charm of lowland Scotland, with its hedges, parks and coppice woods is due to the lay-out designed to integrate sport with farming. It is also true that we owe much of our wealth of Highland wildlife and scenery to the deer forest system, even if our birds of prey suffered disastrously at the hands of game-keepers. Until very recently conservation in the Highlands was a happy accident of isolation.

It brings us face to face with our responsibility for the land, and what happens when we interfere with it. Fortunately, since 1949, we have had the voice of the Nature Conservancy, backed by money and scientific staff to work for our wildlife and establish reserves totalling over 130,000 acres, from relict woodlands, blanket bogs and arctic habitats of the high tops to remote islands of the west which are breeding grounds for Atlantic seals and Leach's petrels.

Knowledge is better than innocence in a land where a romantic vision can too easily obscure the truth. Over twenty years ago Dr F. Fraser Darling wrote:

> The summits of the hills and the inaccessible sea cliffs are as time and evolution made them. The bare hillsides kept bare by burning and the grazing of an artificially large stock of sheep are not wild nature. Wild birch, oak and pine woods without joyous young growth, bereft of their rightful offspring by the all-consuming mouths of sheep and too numerous deer are not wild nature. Where woods have gone there are gashes and landslips on many a hillside, wounds in the earth which are not nature.

The Western Highlands are wonderful, inspiring, but empty if there is no smoke rising from the croft houses or vigorous young children in the schools. Men should be there, not just as tourists, but fulfilling their proper roles.

Let me end by quoting my friend Dr W. J. Eggeling, one time Chief Conservator of Forests in Uganda, and later Tanganyika before becoming Director of the Nature Conservancy in Scotland. Speaking with optimism of the future he enlarged to me as follows:

> The salvation of the Highlands is that so much of it doesn't lend itself to commercial development or argricultural revolution. Even in tourism the climate will dictate developments, which are likely to be geared to a lot of people at short periods. We have to avoid planning from only one point of view. Management is seeing changes as they are taking place, and tracing the present from the

past, and projecting what you see into the future. There is a use for every type of soil, and you must see you do not reduce its fertility.

I have written this book in the hope of sharing with you my enjoyment of the Western Highlands. It is a traveller's tale. Not a guidebook.

CHAPTER ONE

Kintyre and the South-West Hebrides

Kintyre—Colonsay and Oronsay—Islay— Jura—Gigha

Black thunder clouds buried the hills, but on lowland Kintyre the sun was shining and West Loch Tarbert was a mill-pond of fleecy cloud reflections fringed by rich greens and browns. A day to be sailing away from the humid air, and so we were, bound for Colonsay, lying north-west behind Islay and Jura, the most exposed of the Inner Hebrides.

The car ferry is at Kennacraig, near the head of the West Loch, a narrow fjord separating Knapdale on the north from Kintyre on the south, sheltered waters good for seeing birds when the outer sounds are stormy, great northern divers by the dozen in winter, and in summer peppered with tysties, mergansers, skimming flocks of Manx shear-waters and crash-diving gannets.

That August day we looked hard for migrating great shearwaters and travelling skuas, but saw instead a pair of north-flying eagles, the sun gold on their necks, a tawny gloss on the broad aeroplane wings as they planed towards Jura and the quartzite peaks of the 'Paps', gravelly grey above rows of haystacks dotting green fields set round a sparkle of white cottages.

Jura, in August, is sacred to deer stalking and fishing, so this is where we lost a few knickerbocker-clad passengers, dogs at heel, to the waiting estate cars. The most fertile bit of bleak Jura is round the landing place. West round the corner is Islay with only a narrow sound separating it from Jura. You would not guess the fairness of Islay for farming from the landing place at Port Askaig, or suspect the extra-ordinary variety of its bird life. The time was only 8.20 as a big unloading of cars and cargo began, for we had sailed at 6 a.m. and it would take another hour sailing north before we could expect to land on Colonsay.

Colonsay is the most exposed of the Inner Hebrides and in the days preceding 1965 you transferred from below decks into a dory, timing your exit to suit the waves, feeling yourself very lucky if the weather was calm. Indeed you felt lucky to land if it was rough for in that exposed situation there were many occasions when passengers found themselves heading back to Islay. The car ferry began in 1970, and what had been a little-known corner of Utopia was suddenly discovered by campers and caravanners who promptly occupied the most scenic spots. Something had to be done and the Laird did it. He placed a total ban on tents and caravans in order to conserve the beauty of the island for all. On an island as small as Colonsay the principle is a sound one.

Yet your first feeling about Colonsay is likely to be one of disappointment, for the landing at Scalasaig on the east side is among boggy hillocks, the way to the only hotel lying up an undistinctive glen. North over the ridge lies the real Colonsay, and after breakfast we were taking the rough track which climbs north to the rocky jaws of a little pass for the sudden moment of revelation of the Vale of Kiloran, slung like a yellow hammock between hills of purple heather, a small loch for foreground and a curving glimpse of sandy bay beyond the clustering trees of Colonsay House.

This is the valley which the ecologist, Sir F. Fraser Darling, has described as Colonsay's most striking physiographic feature because it is unique. Screened from searing winds by its ridges, it gets the mild Atlantic climate without most of its boisterous disadvantages, and Laird and farmer have taken advantage of it to create a fertile valley across which trail three miles of narrow and shallow loch.

The Vale of Kiloran is the heart of Colonsay, with school, village hall and linear pattern of crofts at the western end. Walk or cycle the 12 miles of road circling from Scalasaig back to Scalasaig, via Machrins, Kilchattan and Kiloran, to see that here, indeed, is a blessed island. The land is good, cattle thrive upon it, the standard of housing is high, yet the population had declined to 130 in 1970 compared to 160 on my last visit five years earlier. Of these the Gaelic speakers numbered about 80, and the primary school roll was 20.

Island friends of mine were pessimistic about the decline, forecasting that the time is rapidly approaching when holiday homes will predominate over those lived in by Colonsay folk, the result of older people dying off and their houses being taken over by the Laird for letting. Nor can the tendency be easily halted when there is so little work due to mechanization of the farms and a run-down of the labour force on the estate. Even the great garden, once a showpiece of the West rivalling Gigha and Inverewe, is being allowed to go wild as the means for upkeep fails.

Colonsay has declined in the 'good times' yet it weathered the potato famine better than any other island of the Hebrides. The 'Old Laird' who died shortly after that bad time, in 1846, saw the greatest days on Colonsay following the Napoleonic wars, and he had seen the effects of too rapid an expansion of population due to high prices for kelp and cattle and more productive agricultural methods. The slump came when free trade knocked the feet from under agriculture.

One crofter's boy whose memories went back to the potato famine wrote down his observations of the way of life of Colonsay. He was Professor McKinnon of Glasgow University, who was reared at Kilchattan when crofters paid their rent in barley and made linen from their own flax, just as they tanned their own cowhide for shoes.

The main foods eaten were rabbits and mutton, he said, with plenty of fish—flounders and saithe—eaten fresh or salted in winter. Fish liver provided oil for the crusie lamp, the wick being provided by the common rush. Seven whisky stills were in busy operation until the Laird unroofed them and brought Customs officers to inspire fear among the islanders. There was always plenty of milk, butter, curds and cream.

Seaweed was still being burned and the resin-like kelp exported to Dumbarton for glass-making, though the price was only a fraction of the £20 a ton obtained during the Napoleonic wars.

The consequence of too many people dependent on a declining agriculture was that the land became so much sub-divided that people were forced to cultivate coarse moor or win a living from fishing. Colonsay had 970 people in the mid-nineteenth century, seven times the population 120 years later. In short Colonsay is such an epitome of the whole story of man in the Western Highlands that I chose to open this book with it.

Take a piece of fairly modern history. The village of Riasg Buidhe is now mere ruins on the roadless shore just north of Scalasaig. You would think it was ancient, but it was evacuated no later than the end of the First World War, in about 1920, when the people were moved nearer the present pier, into the houses of Glas Aird, below the road. In one of these 'new houses' I met a woman of over 90 who recalls rearing a big family in the old village. One of her sons is 75, and strangers lift their eyebrows when he says he is going over to see his mother.

I heard the complete saga of Riasg Buidhe from the late David . Clark. This is how he told it: 'The people were fisherfolk and they lived during the week in a big cave on the west coast of Jura. They would come home with the sail up, or using the oars, when they had made a good haul. The houses had earth floors and thatched roofs. One room would have a few beds in it, and the loft was spread with bracken or twigs for the children.

'But on Sunday you would have thought these men came out of a mansion. Every one of them had a blue suit, with the trousers beautifully creased, and even although they had walked across the rough ground to get to the church there was never a mark on their clothes. Then when the service was over they would walk home, and away would go the blue suit, back into the kist until next Sunday, and on went the navy blue jerseys which were almost a uniform amongst them. It was after the war they stopped going to Jura. Times had changed and the inshore fishing had died out.'

In these not-so-far-off days Colonsay was a remote place served by ships plying from Glasgow to Iona. David Clark's father was pier-master in the days of the *Hebrides* and the *Dunara Castle* and often enough had to sleep in a small shed on the jetty so that he would be ready for the vessel in the middle of the night or the early morning, for there was no such thing as fixed times until the Inner Hebrides service began operating out of West Loch Tarbert.

There is a fine walk from the Riasg Buidhe ruins, north-west over the low hills to Kiloran Bay, or you can continue up the coast past two remarkable woods sprouting up steep faces rising straight from the sea. These trees are small oaks and birches mostly, with some hazel and rowan, true natural woods which have been able to cling here because of their shelter from the Atlantic westerlies. This pristine woodland is being studied by the Nature Conservancy. Seeds have been collected and planted in mainland situations to see how much higher than 20 ft they will grow. By gaining knowledge from these relic woodlands scientists hope to find ways of restoring the lost natural woods of western Scotland.

Wild goats live on the rocks here, descendants of animals once reared for their milk and cheese. Gone wild, they look like shaggy Himalayan thar with swept-back horns. The service they render now is eating grass from ledges where sheep might be tempted and become rock-fast. The herd of fourteen piebalds I saw on this north-east coast were no mean rock climbers.

Balnahard is the most northern farm in the ten-mile length of Colonsay and Oronsay, and if you walk to it along the coast, you can return by a delightful track leading to Kiloran Bay across the shoulder of Carnan Eoin, whose rocky top should be climbed, for at only 470 ft it is the highest peak on the island. There is a large triple cairn for shelter and an eagle's view of Mull to the north, Jura and Islay to the south and Dubh Artach lighthouse and Skerryvore.

Yet it is Colonsay itself which holds the eye more than the distant views, the grey rocks plunging below you to frame the wide curve of Kiloran Bay, behind it the dunes and short turf peppered with grazing cattle stretching to the Vale, the near crofts of Uragaig and the flat fields perched above the sea which are raised beaches of a former shore.

Easy to imagine, from this commanding position, the post-glacial epoch when the sea level stood 140 ft higher than it does now and made Colonsay four islands. The richest land was under water, the whole Vale of Kiloran, much of Beinn Bhreac, and the land between Scalasaig and Machrins. But all that was before the coming of the Azilian people who lived at the southern end of Colonsay, across the Strand in Oronsay.

We know of these strand loopers of roughly 9,000 years ago from what they left behind them in what have been described as 'the finest Mesolithic sites in Europe'. The kitchen middens which have yielded the finds lay buried under an accumulation of sand built up over the thousands of years since the sea retreated from them. Sites which have been excavated lie fairly close to Seal Cottage.

The people who made these dumps were hunters, living on the shore, using bone harpoons and deer-horn tools. They are the first known men to have colonized Scotland, and it is thought they reached the Western Highlands from Asia and Europe. Bone pins indicate that they wore clothes, just as the deposits of their middens show they gathered limpets in vast quantities and killed birds, including the great auk.

Colonsay is a museum of man, Mesolithic on Oronsay, Neolithic at Kiloran Bay where flint tools have been found in a cave. Then we move to the Christian period, and the graves of the Viking raiders who dominated the West for 400 years. In the grave of a Norseman who was buried with his sword, spear, axes, shield and boat was found a coin, a half-farthing of Vigmond, Archbishop of York, with the date 831–845 on it.

Oronsay has some ecclesiastical fame, for this was where St Columba landed on his mission voyage to Scotland before sailing on to Iona. The year was 563 and the story goes that St Columba passed on because he could see Ireland from the highest hill. The Priory ruins you see today date from 1380 and are on the site of a sixth-century Columban foundation.

These monastic ruins are the best in the West Highlands, with cloisters featuring low pointed arches of a style said to be peculiar to the eastern Mediterranean. The Great Cross, bearing a carved figure of Christ, was erected to the memory of Prior Colin who died in 1510. Unfortunately the Priory was plundered for its stones to build the steadings of the adjacent farm. An even more uncivilized act was the destruction of Kiloran Abbey to build the present Colonsay House. Oran was the name of a follower of St Columba who landed with him on Oronsay. In time he became a saint, and is now immortalized in the name Kiloran Bay.

Oronsay is cut off from Colonsay for two hours on each side of high tide, and sandshoes on barefeet are advised for protection against razor shells, especially before the water has properly drained from the strand. Look out for a weed-covered cross half-way over, marking the boundary of a sanctuary. Once over that boundary within the sanctuary a criminal could consider himself free if he stayed for a year and a day. Columban times were more generous than ours. Crossing from Colonsay, a good landmark is the 'elephant's trunk rock' so called because of its undoubted resemblance to a hanging trunk.

The character of Oronsay is quite different from anything on

Colonsay, flatter and more oceanic. The island airfield is here, in use for charter flights and air ambulance. Southward Oronsay trails away in some rocky skerries known as Eilean nan Ron–the island of seals—and I had the good luck to be taken out there by Neil Ban and Andrew McNeil of Oronsay after waiting two days for an October south-wester to stop whipping the white caps off the waves breaking between us and the skerries. A mistake of judgement here and you could find yourself heading for America on a tossing sea.

We made it when the tide turned, climbing out of the boat up weed-covered reefs to a grassy top. We stumbled on the first seal cow before she knew it, not quietly enough unfortunately, for in an instant she leapt nine feet into the water, coming out of it with a great bow-wave to bounce up the beach like a rubber ball, her great hands and blubbery undersides slapping on the rocks as she wheeled about and took up a defensive position on what we now saw was a little cream-coloured pup.

Not to disturb her unduly we moved on, and soon found ourselves in a nursery of Atlantic seals of all ages and sizes: little puppies not long born who could hardly lift themselves on their arms, yet putting up a fierce show of anger, mouthing threats with toothless gums; others at the well-covered sleepier stage who looked at us from large watery eyes but were too contented to move; others were shedding their baby hair to reveal the hard blue pelt of adolescence, reached at two-and-a-half weeks. Hard to believe that the helpless pups weighing 30 lbs. would look like these 90 pounders in less than 21 days, thanks to a diet of mother's milk several times richer than cow's milk. The pups were certainly well insulated. The heat between the flippers was such that it was like putting your hand on a hot-water bottle, which is what a thick layer of blubber and a fast heart beat of 170 to the minute can do to alleviate the Atlantic cold.

Some of the month-old adolescents were playing in the rock pools, somersaulting, floating belly-up, or poking out curious noses to see what these strange objects were above them. They were willing to play a game and have their backs stroked, at which they would almost leap out of the water and come back for more, making growling noises. At four weeks they carried so much blubber they were as buoyant as corks and from a deep dive would pop up to the surface with a comical suddenness.

There was plenty of roaring and wailing from the adult bulls and cows with the mating urge. You could see them rearing up at each other, whiskery face to whiskery face, in a mixture of aggression and love. Spent bulls may be down in weight by 300 lbs by the time they go back to the sea, but keen fights between old and new bulls sometimes take place. We saw one such fight, and it resulted in the harem of cows getting a new master.

Two quarter-ton giants were wailing at each other, mouth to mouth, when the fresh bull lunged and gripped the other by the neck, drawing a spurt of blood. Instantly the old bull in possession made an agile twist and gripped the attacker's hind flipper, hanging on to it despite retaliatory bites from the other. Then both drew back, flippers raised like boxers, each blotched with blood.

Then the fresh bull renewed the attack. The old animal tried to get away, only to be bitten in the rear each time he turned away. The fight was over, and when the winning bull finally let the vanquished go, it turned over on its side and fell fast asleep. Barnacle geese, newly arrived from Greenland, were yapping like dogs as a flight passed over our rowing boat, marking time until we pulled away, then down they went, rocking the air out of their wings as they whiffled down to stand on the grassy crown on the island of seals, just the sight to put inspirational period to the day.

Islay is as green as the best of Ireland, except in the rugged north and south-east, which have more the look of Jura and share the same quartzite formation. Sanaigmore in the extreme north-west is one of my favourite places. The view stretches uninterruptedly to Colonsay and the Ross of Mull, with eastward the Garvellachs and Seil Island. Here, too, are fine bird cliffs where, if you have a head for heights, you can traverse airy ledges on sound rock and almost rub noses with razorbills who merely turn inquiring heads, seldom moving off to reveal the single pointed egg which seems too large for such a small bird. No nest, just a spotted egg on a bare rock, a top-storey for quiet birds with noisy neighbours below in screaming kittiwakes and 'gurring' guillemots.

The special bird of this place and other sea cliffs of Islay is the chough whose sound is an explosive 'tee-ah', more dynamic than the sound of any jackdaw and a flight to match: powerful down-strokes and sudden dives as the wings are thrown back to bullet down, then spread out the brakes and soar up again. One I watched did a vertical dive of 200 ft, suddenly flattening out to adhere a moment on a ledge then it was off again. But in that second I saw another chough dart to it, take food from its red curved bill and scramble back again into a hole.

Strange that the chough stronghold should be here when it has disappeared from the rest of the British coast. Yet perhaps not so strange when Ireland is only 23 miles across the water and there are good colonies of choughs in Donegal. Gordon Booth, a resident ornithologist, tells me the Islay population is holding its own very nicely, and long may it continue. One pair actually bred in a space between the stones of a house on a moor.

Gordon Booth is a retired cloth manufacturer from Wharfdale, and it was with him I went to see the geese on a December visit in 1971. Gordon and his wife had fallen in love with Islay and decided to make it their permanent home. 'I would say that the two years I have been here have been the happiest of my life. We don't want to leave Islay even for a weekend. There's so much to see and do here there just isn't enough time to do it. The folk are such good company. Conversation is still an art here.'

Gordon is a dedicated ornithologist who has worked for many years with Peter Scott on geese, and he was able to tell me that from his counts he could say that there were over 16,000 barnacle geese and 3,000 Greenland white-fronted geese that winter. He took me to the Gruinart flats and Ardnave where most of the birds congregate.

I have studied barnacle geese in Greenland and I have had the thrill of seeing them in their wintering grounds on Islay on other occasions. It is a thrill which never fades, for nowhere else in the world can so many barnacle geese be seen in one place at one time as here. Motoring along the green bowl of the flats we were surrounded by them, like mobile grey rugs edging away from us whenever we stopped the car. Glad to record, for the farmers' sakes, they were nicely shared out over the best grazing acres. In fact the geese can be prevented from being a nuisance by merely breaking up their packs with a dog.

The massive edging-away movement became alarm when we got down from the car and the few dog-like yelps became one clamouring wave of high-pitched sound as thousands of birds took the air. All we needed was the sun to break from the obscuring clouds, and we got it, a flash to light the snow-white cheeks of the barnacles and show off the ebony chests and dove-grey backs of birds on the ground and in the air. By contrast the Greenland whitefronts showed off their zebra stripes and patch of facial snow round the base of the bill. Farms, cattle, water hollows, reedbeds and green hills shone as we edged along slowly in the car, stopping to listen to the piping of golden plover mingling with curlew cries.

I remembered one late April evening on Jura when I had an unforgettable sight. As here the sun was low, sometimes obscured by cloud, then it would burst forth, gilding each house and tree with golden light, making of the tiny fields a neat quilt of delicate beauty against the tawny moors. Then came the touch that transformed the moment to a special place in the memory, as the sun lit against the pale blue of the Paps a great arrowhead of streaming birds, each a flake of black and white, the whole gaggle chorusing wildly as they flew north towards the land of the midnight sun. The barnacles were off to their nesting grounds, Iceland first stop, then across the Denmark Strait to Greenland, to lay eggs within a week of arrival.

Motoring on the 75 miles of driving roads of Islay you get the impression of a wide countryside of flattish fields peppered with far too many ruins, representing, I suppose, the drop of population from 10,000 a hundred years ago to something around 4,000 today, with most of them concentrated in the whisky distilling regions of Port Askaig, Port Ellen, Bowmore and Bruichladdich. The interior is thinly populated and clearly there could be a vast expansion of forestry if it was wanted.

Conditions have vastly improved on Islay since Sir Frank Fraser Darling's *West Highland Survey*, an essay in human ecology published in 1954. In it Darling had said that social life on Islay was at a low ebb, that standards of husbandry were very low, and he had remarked on the decline in Gaelic culture due to a steady drift to the towns.

The population has stabilized, farms have been modernized, there is an island creamery which collects the milk and makes Islay cheese, but at the time of writing its future is in doubt because interest in dairying has declined due to the profit from raising suckler calves and selling them for finishing away from the island. The cattle population was estimated to be about 13,000 in 1972. Shared out among 500 farms it is not as much as it sounds, but the healthy aspect is the lowering of the ratio of sheep to cattle. Their trading organization is called 'Islay Farmers' which runs a bulk-buying shop, for household goods as well as farming stuffs. An appointed manager handles the selling side of the beasts.

It was a travelling salesman who told me: 'There is plenty of money to go round on Islay. I know, for I am seeing the whole population, and there are no poor people as in the old days. We're getting on for a million unemployed in Britain, but there are only one or two drawing dole money here. See how the distilleries have extended their warehouses!'

The different peat flavours of the water make each Islay whisky distinctive, though not all of the eight distilleries produce a brand for sale, most of it being used only for blending. The secret of Islay whisky has to do with the size of the still, which hasn't changed since ancient times despite more modern methods. About 250 men are employed on shift work which is a small number when you consider that there is not a Scotch blend which does not contain some Islay malt.

The tourist trade has boomed since the introduction of car ferries on the Islay run. On Gigha and Colonsay you hardly need a car. Even on Jura it has a limited value when most of it is roadless. On Islay you have to be mobile to make use of the coastal variety of both sides of the Rhinns, or explore the Mull of Oa to Claggan Bay in the south-east where the road ends. Down in that corner of the south-east stands the greatest of Islay's many archaeological treasures, the 9-ft sculptured cross of Kildalton dating from the eighth century.

It stands outside Kildalton Chapel, whose tiny outside font never dries up. The embossed cross was cut and carved by one of the Columban monks, it is believed. Chiselled from a single piece of stone and showing Christ in glory it is the supreme masterpiece of its kind, solid and yet delicate, to last the ages and act upon the mind.

There is an Irish flavour about the villages on Islay with their whitewash and straggling lay-out above the sea. Port Ellen is the most southerly and connected by straight road to Bowmore which has an altogether neater lay-out and the focal point of a circular church on a hill. Bowmore looks west across the broad sea inlet of Loch Indaal, which is one of the best places in the Hebrides for birds.

The local bird man here is Robert Hodkinson, a general merchant, whose home is a war-time NAAFI overlooking the loch. Standing with him at his door in December we looked out on a glassy surface thickly spattered with birds, nearest to us a flock of over 500 scaup in a tight feeding raft, while out from them were little parties of goldeneye, wigeon, teal, mallard, eiders, mergansers and separate herds of mute and whooper swans.

'You should be here at dawn,' enthused Robert Hodkinson, 'when the barnacle geese start flighting. You can't lie on when you have that alarm clock ringing in your ears. I do my morning birding here without moving. See the flock of twites on the wires there, like slim sparrows. And just below you can always see waders.' As he spoke we looked down on foraging turnstones, oyster catchers, redshanks, curlews and gulls.

Motor east from Bowmore and you are into the fertile schist and limestone soils in a soft scenery of woods and broad fields, yet there is sterile quartzite on each side of Ballygrant, a relatively short distance away. These hills are really an extension of the Paps of Jura and must have been linked to them before ice-age glaciers dug the channel covered now by the Sound of Islay.

And as in Jura these hills are used as deer forest giving fine stalking though the highest hills are only 1,500 ft. The big royal stags are easy to see in the winter time, especially if you contact the head keeper at Ballygrant and get him to take you up to the place where he feeds them on crushed maize. On my visit the best was a thirteen pointer, straight-backed and carrying its head high, leaping the fence into the park and trotting with high steps that made it look as if on springs. These animals are conserved to improve the stock, and not shot for the trophy.

North of Ballygrant there is a link with other Royal heads at Loch Finlaggan occupying a mile-long trench in the hills, the home of the Lords of the Isles who ruled from a castle on an island. The skeletal gable-ends are still visible, and near it is the 'Council Isle' where underlords of the Isles met when summoned by their king.

But Islay requires a book of its own if anything like justice is to be done to all its parts, from the hanging jaw of the Mull of Oa across the open mouth of Laggan Bay and Loch Indaal to the long muzzle of the Rhinns. Without the big sheltering headlands this west coast would be bleak and windswept. Without the eastern hills you would not have the trees, for Islay is an oceanic island, more so than most in the Hebrides. But cross the Sound of Islay and it is a different story.

It was a Jura man who lured me to his island, rejecting my statement that it looked wild and barren. 'You come with me. You will love Jura for the birds alone. We have every kind there. And bleak! There used to be over a thousand people on Jura and the shore and lower hills are still green with the fields they left behind. There are only about 200 living there now. Every loch carries fish, and we can splash-net for salmon. With the boat we can visit islands and skerries where seals breed. The boat is a cabin-cruiser and we will sail from the Clyde, through the Kyles of Bute, Loch Fyne, the Crinan Canal, and over the Sound to Jura.'

We sailed from Largs on what proved to be the last day of a remarkable April heat-wave, and lighthouses were stabbing the darkness of Jura's Sound as we steered for Small Isles Bay and Dan McKellar's cottage on Feolin. His navigation could scarcely have been bettered. When we switched on our searchlight its beam picked up the white square of his house. So I made an unconventional arrival in Jura.

Showers of rain next morning with sun flashes from racing cumulus flocks was return to more normal April weather. The air seemed filled with bird songs from mingling skylarks and willow warblers to the shrilling of wading birds. We headed north into a land and sea-scape in poster colour, vivid greens, blue sea, clouds dabbing the sky like cotton wool, the lighthouse which had guided our landfall a pencil of dazzling white.

Every little inlet held flocks of eiders, the ivory drakes neck-jerking and bobbing as they cooed in unison. The joy of life was in the air in the cries of peewits, the shrilling of curlews and oyster catchers, the drumming of snipe and whisking flocks of burbling golden plover.

The friendly crofters were busy in the fields, planting potatoes and harrowing the corn seed, a full two weeks earlier than usual. No one could have called the scene bleak: a clachan of houses, some gleaming white, slate-roofed, some grey stone and thatched; sloping furrows of ploughland and a sprinkling of new-born lambs in the new grass; and over them the Bens of Jura above the heathery moor. Long strips of tawny light raced over the island, gleaming bright as amber then darkening with the shadow.

Alas, this bit of beauty is confined to the south-eastern corner where the quartzite gives way to kindlier rocks, hornblende, phyllitic and mica schist. As Sir F. Fraser Darling has said, Jura can scarcely avoid being a problem. It is deer forest, which means that visitors are less welcome in the shooting season than on other islands of the group.

Not that there is much scope for pleasurable walking on the hills for they are too rough, though Ghlas Bheinn rising 1,839 ft above Small Isles Bay is easy enough. We had cold clarity for our climb, seeing the map spring to life as Arran rose beyond the long arm of Kintyre and northwards the twin peaks of Cruachan pricked the horizon. Below us was Islay, the Rhinns deep-cut by silver lochs, almost an island on its own.

Jura, too, is almost two islands divided at mid-length by the west-cutting Loch Tarbert. We explored this by boat. Barren as is the interior, everywhere on the coast is the evidence of former lazybeds where hundreds of antler-less deer were roaming. This side of the island facing Colonsay is famous for its caves, of sizes and shapes to suit everybody. It would be nice to know which one the fishermen of Colonsay used as their base. Burial parties en route to Iona were known to use one with an altar stone known to this day as *Uamh Muinntir.*

Jura, however unfavoured, had a special geographical significance to the Islay folk, for by ferrying their cattle across at Port Askaig they could walk them up the coast to Lagg, or to the very north point of Jura, and get a short sea crossing to Knapdale, thus bringing the passes of Loch Fyne and Loch Awe within easy reach. Ferry records kept from 1801 to 1807 show that the average number of beasts crossing from Islay to Jura en route to market was 2,640 at roughly £7 each.

John MacCulloch witnessed the ferry crossing in 1824 and wrote:

The shore was covered with cattle; and while some were collected in groups under the trees and rocks, crowding to avoid the hot rays of a July evening, others were wading in the sea to shun the flies, some embarking, and another set swimming onshore from the ferry boats; while the noise of the drovers and the boatmen, and all the bustle and vociferation which whisky did not tend to diminish, were re-echoed from hill to hill, contrasting strangely with the silence and solitude of the surroundings.

7   *The Great Cross of Oronsay, one of the two finest in Scotland*

The next leg of the journey across the five-mile-wide Sound of Jura has been well described by road engineer Joseph Mitchell:

> At last we cleared the land, and got into the channel. How the wind did roar, and how the cattle struggled to get their heads free! The extent of sail we carried was forcing the bow of the boat too deep into the sea, and there was a fear of being swamped.

The immediate destination of the drovers was said to be the market of Kilmichael-Glassary, then on they would march to Falkirk, taking a week or a fortnight en route.

The northern passage from the tip of Jura to Craignish point must have been the trickiest crossing, for the whirlpool of Corrievreckan is just round the corner, and ahead was the north end of the Dorus Mor where the tide races roar like rivers at flood and ebb. Corrievreckan is no more than a narrow strait between Jura and the near island of Scarba to its north. The turbulence is caused by a subterranean rock deflecting the racing waters, to collide at an angle with the top layer of current, so you have a boil of water like an upside down waterfall, as if gravity had gone into reverse. You can see it well from the Jura or Scarba shores. This was the 'overland' route which the Islay people wanted to restore as the best route to the mainland. And, who knows, it may come yet. Meantime, however, the mainland terminal for beasts and travellers is still West Loch Tarbert, and it is to the village of Tarbert I shall now return you, situated on a narrow neck of land on a gateway to the Firth of Clyde and the Western Islands. But for that little neck of land Kintyre would be an island separated from Knapdale by a narrow strait from the Sound of Gigha through West Loch Tarbert to Loch Fyne.

No other region of the west is richer in history, for it can be said that hereabouts the Scots assumed identity as a people. The Picts who fought the Romans are a mysterious people. But while they were engaged in driving out the enemy around AD 250, a tribe of Gaels known as Scots sailed from Ireland to Kintyre and using the long sea lochs established themselves round a rocky hillock on Crinan Moss, calling their new kingdom Dalriada after their home in County Antrim.

Scotland at that time was known as Alban. At the death of the Antrim King Erc, 250 years later, three of his sons took a more firm

8   *Loch Fyne, near Inveraray in Argyllshire, Cowal peaks distant*

grip on the original colonization. Angus held Islay. Lorn went north, and the Firth of Lorn still bears his name. Fergus, who took Kintyre, Knapdale and Cowal, outlived the other two and united the whole into a Dalriada which now stretched from the Mull of Kintyre to Ardnamurchan Point. Alban of the Picts and Dalriada of the Scots became Scotland when the Celtic King, Kenneth MacAlpin, conquered his neighbours in 843, at the time the Norsemen were settling in the Hebrides.

The Viking nuisance had been endured for over 300 years by the time Malcolm III was on the throne and fighting off other invaders of his domain, the English. To concentrate on one front he made the young Norwegian king, Magnus Barelegs, an offer: to take any island of the west he could reach by ship with his rudder in place. By couching it in these terms he thought he had protected his mainland, and off he went to war.

The wily Magnus put a more liberal interpretation on that definition of an island when he came to Tarbert in 1093. He knew very well that only a short neck of land separated Loch Fyne on the Clyde from the deep bite of the West Loch, not a long haul for strong men. So he sat in his galley and let himself be pulled across, thus duping Malcolm. Nor could the Scottish king take reprisal for he was killed in battle that November.

The Scottish reprisal had to wait until a young man called Somerled grew up to become King of Argyll in 1130. He was a descendant of Con of the Hundred Battles. The showdown came on 6 January 1156. He met the Norse galleys with a fleet of his own and drove them from Kintyre and the southern Hebrides. The battle took place off Islay's west coast. Somerled set up his kingly house on Islay after this and was killed by Malcolm IV in 1164.

Tarbert is best viewed from the ivy-covered ruin on the hill called Bruce's Castle, though it dates beyond that time to the early kings of Dalriada. Bruce did not arrive until 1326 to rebuild it into a fortress. And to show the independent chiefs who was king he had his ships hauled across like Magnus Barelegs before. In fact he set going a custom which lasted until the end of the eighteenth century for ships unwilling to round the exposed Mull of Kintyre. The custom ended with the opening of the Crinan Canal.

A coastal sweep by car round Kintyre is very nearly possible today, with only one small gap on the west coast south of Machrihanish. However it should be lengthened to take in the Isle of Gigha (pronounced Geeah) by leaving your car at Tayinloan and crossing on the regular passenger ferry. The fast road runs down the West Loch and over the ups and downs by Clachan to a turning at Tayinloan leading to the jetty on its spit of white sand.

Most day-trippers go to see the famous gardens, sheltered by fine trees and bursting with colour on a gentle hill. Palm trees growing in the open testify to the mildness of the climate here. Even the fields climb to nearly the top of the highest hill, admittedly only 331 ft. There is only six miles of driving road running north to south, virtually the length of the island, yet it is impossible to explore the joys of this narrow island in less than a fortnight.

You see why the Norsemen were fond of anchoring their fleet here, on a Piccadilly Circus of seaways, but with a disadvantage of having no perfect harbour. Yet Gigha has two piers, one in the south-east and the other at the northern tip. My own favourite place on the island is Port Mor, another Tarbert, almost cut off from the rest of Gigha by incutting bays. Here is a perfect bit of Hebridean scene, curves of white sand, rocky shores, nesting birds, great boulders, cliffs and special places beloved of otters.

Sitting above the clear green water I have watched a dog otter swimming as if in an aquarium as it probed about in the yellow seaweed, then, catching a crab, swim ashore with it, whiskery face no more than ten yards away as it laid the crab down, stretched itself out in a comfortable position for eating, belly down, take the crab gently in its mouth, and with one crunch crack it into fragments. Then using the two front feet like a knife and fork proceed to eat it daintily. You felt the only thing that was missing was a napkin.

This spot in May and early June epitomizes all that is best in the Hebrides, rioting seapinks among the rocks, yellow flags in the wet spots, primroses and blue hyacinths still blooming on the banks, buzzards on the crags, terns, oyster catchers, ringed plovers on the shores, and in the bays black guillemots, eiders, sheld duck and maybe a red-throated or a great northern diver.

Back on the mainland at Tayinloan, you are less than half way to the Mull of Kintyre which is a full 40 miles from Tarbert. To get to it means passing east to Campbeltown on its deep bite of loch, a royal burgh with the most superb of anchorages. Easy to reach by ship and air from Glasgow the 6,500 people who live here are not isolated. There is even a car-ferry to Ireland in summer, to Cushindall in the north. Western Ferries brought back the ancient link with Antrim.

The grey town has a thriving air with well stocked shops and harbour full of boats, distilleries, creamery and tourist traffic. Davaar Island, accessible at low tide, is a popular place of pilgrimage to see a painting of the Crucifixion in one of the seven caves of this island. But find out first about the tides, lest you be stranded on the island.

You should go on to Southend and climb the little rocky knobble called Dunaverty which used to have a castle but now has only a grassy top above a three-sided cliff. From here the Antrim hills are only eleven miles away, and if the day be clear you may even see the Isle of Man. Reflect as you stand here on the events of 300 years ago when 300 MacDonalds and MacDougalls held the castle on this hill-top against ten times that number of Leslie's Covenanting army, until lack of water drove them to parley for terms.

They surrendered, to be massacred by the troops waiting for them. Only one boy was spared. Leslie totally destroyed the castle that had been a fortress for a thousand years, and of its remains there is now no sign.

The effect of this war, and the plague which followed Leslie's troops into Kintyre, left Argyll master of a depopulated land. He did not want trouble-making Highlanders, so he introduced Low-landers from Ayrshire and Renfrew to his land, good farmers who quickly saw the possibilities of the fertile parts of this rich peninsula, developing the coastal fishing at the same time. The fishing has much declined since then; but the magnificent fields of cattle and good crops south of Campbeltown are more typical of the Lowlands than the Highlands, and a testimony to the Ayrshire farming methods. There is plenty of woodland shelter too.

The road north back to Tarbert by the east coast is slower and narrower than the west road, which is a good job, for there is much to enjoy: the hills of Arran just across the Kilbrennan Sound to the east; Saddell with its sixteenth-century castle and old chapel where Somerled the conqueror of the Vikings was laid to rest in 1164; Carradale and Skipness lying just off the main road but not to be missed for their snug beauty of situation, Carradale with its two harbours, fishing fleet and fine salmon river, Skipness with such a solid castle that you would hardly believe it dates from the thirteenth century. The once fine chapel built in the same period has not lasted so well.

In a tour round of Kintyre you have much to think about: the nature of the peninsula and of Magnus Barelegs who won it by his trick; of Somerled who broke Norwegian power in the west and whose house ruled from Islay, maintaining peace and prosperity for the next 300 years. But their power and independence was resented and feared by the Crown, and it fell to James IV to break it without substituting anything stabilizing in its place. So the clans reverted to internecine feuding which was to last from 1493 until 1609 when James VI had enough political sense to get order restored.

The mainstay of life today in the country I have been describing is farming, fishing, whisky distilling, tourism, some forestry, and estate work connected with deer stalking and shooting. Tarbert, with its ferry connections and the increased interest in yachting, has grown to be something of a centre, with good shops and plenty of bed-and-breakfast facilities of high quality. The modern fishing fleet and the active life of the quay make it a lively place to stay, with Arran and the Kyles of Bute just round the corner and connected by daily boat service.

People today wonder why a canal was never cut through at Tarbert to link the East and West Loch in a mile of artificial waterway. It was considered, but abandoned in favour of a more northern cut from Loch Gilp to Loch Crinan because the saving of sea miles by the Crinan passage would be considerably greater, 75 miles as compared to only 55. So, instead of a short cut at Tarbert, a long cut of nine miles between Ardrishaig and Crinan was opened in 1801 at a cost of £140,610.

And it is to Scotland's Panama we go now, not so fanciful a description if you think of the Mull of Kintyre as a miniature Cape Horn, its narrow neck pierced by Loch Gilp in the south and Loch Crinan in the north, offering a sheltered passage through woods as opposed to the detour east of Ireland and north by the Sounds of Gigha and Jura.

CHAPTER TWO

Dalriada, Lorn and Cowal

The Crinan Canal—Loch Fyne and Dalriada— Inveraray—the Arrochar Alps and Cowal

Until you have sailed from the Clyde by the Kyles of Bute to Loch Fyne it is hard to appreciate the complications of the west coast. This was our route to Jura by cabin cruiser as described in the last chapter. We were heading for Ardrishaig at the southern entrance to the Crinan Canal, and as we chugged along on a glass-calm sea past Loch Striven and Loch Ridden and southward to round Ardlamont Point I began to understand why so many peaks and headlands have Norse names. They would be vital navigational aids on such a segmented coast with further openings from the Clyde estuary to Loch Long, Loch Goil and the Gareloch.

A straight line from Largs goes right through West Loch Tarbert to Islay, but the Norse galleys had to round the Mull of Kintyre when it came to doing battle, and it is appropriate that it was at Largs that their power was finally broken. In that 1263 battle with King Alexander III the fleet was a vital factor, especially when the Scots were gaining the upper hand on land. It was Norse bad luck that a fierce storm should blow up and damage their fleet, forcing them to withdraw. And never again did they sail back. It was the end for them, and defeated King Hakon died in Orkney three months later.

Seven hundred years later the Crinan Canal was seen to be the solution to the problem of the Mull of Kintyre. Ironically, however, it was built just 50 years too soon. Just a bit more delay and it would have been planned for steamships, but the Government of the time were rightly depressed by the state of the west coast fisheries and agreed that a canal offering a direct route from Loch Fyne to the

38

western seas would save more than a long and dangerous voyage for sailing ships. It could be the means of bringing prosperity to the Highlands.

The financing of the work was left to private enterprise, such public-spirited individuals as the Duke of Argyll, the Earl of Breadalbane, the Marquis of Lorn and the Provost of Glasgow subscribing money to get a beginning made in 1793 under John Rennie. Rennie's estimated cost of £107,000 was so far out that the canal would never have been finished but for the Government's stepping in with £25,000. But even with that additional loan the canal could not be satisfactorily completed. It was opened in an unfinished state, with such difficult bends and rocky corners in its western sector that shipping was and is still endangered.

The workmanship was bad, banks and masonry leaked and reservoirs collapsed. The Government put more money into it, with little result until around 1820 when the Caledonian Canal opened. Then the Crinan enjoyed a period of increasing usefulness, handling vessels coming down from Loch Linnhe and the Firth of Lorn. Prosperity was short-lived, however, for the steamship had arrived, and few of the new vessels trading with the west could pass through the small locks of the canal. The Crinan white elephant became Crown property just 52 years from the date of the first loan. It had failed to help the fishing trade or alleviate the poverty and isolation of the isles.

Queen Victoria went through it in August 1847 and wrote of the passage:

We glided along very smoothly, and the views of the hills—the range of Cruachan—were very fine indeed; but the eleven locks we had to go through were tedious, and instead of the passage lasting one hour and a half it lasted upwards of two hours and a half.

In fact there are 15 locks, and the passage took our small cabin cruiser five hours from Ardrishaig to Crinan, climbing at one point from 32 ft to 64 ft, to drop back to 32 ft in only a mile-and-a-quarter costing eight locks. How much better it would have been to dispense with these eight locks by merely digging down an extra 32 feet, thus reducing the summit height of the canal by that amount. Vessels which have to wait for the tide can expect to take 12 hours to cover the nine miles of the canal; 88 ft by 20 ft is the maximum size of craft taken.

The compensation is the beauty of the journey round a succession of leafy curves, each bringing a new prospect into view, of lawn-like turf, Forestry Commission woods of larch and spruce, well-kept gardens glowing with rock plants in blue, pink and yellow, and the descent to the sea in a great alluvial flat known as the Moss of Crinan crowned by the rocky fort of Dunadd. In April the passage resounded with birds, the crying of curlews, the drumming of snipe, the triple calls of redshank and the shrilling of oyster catchers.

Crinan itself is a green haven with a sweep of bay opening out to the Sound of Jura, with little rocklets of islands standing north to Corryvreckan and the Dorus Mor—the Great Gate to the Firth of Lorne and the Hebrides.

The Irish tribe known as the Scots, when they made their fortress at Dunadd, chose a rocky height of great strategic importance at the junction of Lorn and Kintyre, their provinces. So let's take a look at Dunadd, where the Stone of Destiny was first kept, the same that now sits in Westminster Abbey. Driving up from Tarbert you take the Oban road at Lochgilphead, following the Crinan Canal to a point about a mile west of the forestry village of Kilmichael Glassary. An 'Ancient Monument' signpost points the way through a farm-yard.

The climb to the summit is a sharp 160 ft, not much of a height, but the top commands every approach to it over a wide range of country-side, the Moss with its winding river banks dotted with cattle, and to the south-east the Paps of Jura, with the twin peaks of Cruachan to the north-east pin-pointing the direction of Loch Awe. There are three interesting rock carvings on top associated with the inauguration of the kings of Dalriada. One is a cut-out the shape of a human foot. Beside it is a hollow in the shape of a basin. The third is an engraving of a wild boar. Only three such carvings exist in Scotland. Fergus who brought the Stone of Destiny, which was Jacob's pillow at Bethel, probably sat on it, placing his foot on the cut-out human foot after a ceremonial washing with the water from the little rock basin.

A glance at an Ordnance Survey map will disclose an astonishing galaxy of ancient monuments: chambered cairns, monoliths, stone circles, earthworks, castle remains, inscribed rocks and forts in which the stonework has been vitrified by fire. An archaeological explorer can have a feast, especially as many of these monuments have to be sought out—no well-beaten trail leads to them. But the range is from Neolithic times to the Christian period, with its magnificent Celtic crosses as in Kilmartin churchyard. A cross section of the best of everything may be found only two miles north of Dunadd, the huge burial cairn at Nether Largie and the Templewood stone circle. The Ministry of Works guidebook to the ancient monuments of Scotland is an inexpensive and invaluable work.

In the last chapter I recalled the cattle-droving days. By following the droving routes which were in use even into this century through the hills we can gain a good idea of Dalriadan topography. There were two landing points, at Craignish just across the loch from Crinan, and at Keills to the south, near the mouth of Loch Sween. Heading for Falkirk, the Craignish cattle would swing round by the west end of Loch Awe, while the Keills drove came by the wooded shores of Loch Sween and along the edge of Crinan Moss to Kilmichael-Glassary, and north-east by the River Add. Both droves converged eastwards on the way to Inveraray.

The motorist who has been with me so far has a choice of reaching Inveraray by Loch Awe and Glen Aray, or returning to Lochgilp-head and following the Loch Fyne coast to the county town of Argyll. Taking the sea loch past Crarae and Furnace, look out for a little clachan of houses on the hill-pass to Inveraray. Stop here if you would see a unique Museum of Folk and Farming Life, for this is a complete settlement whose last occupant moved out only in 1954, and it gives good insight into the communal agricultural life which existed here not so long ago.

Remember too that this is on the old drove road. The signpost still points 'Public Footpath to Lochaweside', and even if the Forestry Commission have turned part of it into a road it is still a wild route, needing careful map reading, as does the western branch to Kil-michael-Glassary, much of it now afforested.

At Auchindrain you learn how families worked together on the land, sharing common grazing and taking their cattle to the shielings in summer. The field dykes of the arable are still visible, and in the houses and byres and stables you can see the furniture and the implements which were the background of their daily lives. The

quality of the articles shows that they were made to last. The loom
for example, which has been weaving tartans for 250 years, is still
sound.

Loch Fyne of the low grassy hills and wooded shores wears, you
feel, almost too civilized a look to be in the Highlands, but even so it
is a surprise to find at Inveraray a Highland town of Georgian design,
well described by the Wordsworths, who visited it in 1803, as truly
festive in appearance. Perhaps it is even more dazzling today, with
the 1820 courthouse added and fine restoration work carried out by
the Ministry of Works who took over the town at valuation from the
present Duke of Argyll.

The new town of Inveraray dates from after the '45 when roads
were first driven into the Highlands. Until then Inveraray lay half a
mile north of its present position and was a sprawl of thatched houses
with no less than 43 taverns serving the herring-fishing fleet. The
River Aray ran through it, and above was the tower of the Campbell
castle, built by Colin of Loch Awe in 1415, and same who was known
as *Cailean Mor*, the great warrior.

The Campbells had flourished in association with Bruce and Wal-
lace. Colin's son became the first earl some 42 years after the first
castle at Inveraray was built. The tenth earl became the first duke in
1701. True to their interests the second duke supported the Union of
Scotland and England in 1707, and in the 1715 rising had routed the
Jacobites at Sheriffmuir. A field-marshal, his service in Marlborough's
war had paid off.

Inveraray was planned by the third duke with the help of his close
friend Lord Milton and the architect Roger Morris. They designed a
new castle on the old site above the mouth of the Aray but planned the
new town half a mile away on Gallows Foreland Point, arranging the
buildings to be in squares within a polygon to use the shape of the
site to best advantage. John Adams, brother to the famous Robert,
supervised much of the work, and his town house and great inn are
still the dominant features. In fact these were the only two public
buildings which had been constructed when the old duke died.

The fourth duke let things lapse, the new castle was unfinished,
the old town still sprawled beneath it, and the new town had its
planned avenue with Adam buildings on each side of it and some
new estate houses built along the Gallowgate. The fifth duke, with

Robert Mylne as architect, finished the castle, built the two-arched bridge over the Aray and demolished the old town as the new sprang up.

All this was done in the 1770s and '80s as Mylne put in his main street parallel to the great avenue, built the fine facade of the east side, and oversaw private buildings. The harling of the houses with their slate roofs must have seemed grand indeed to the peasantry outside, who still lived in rough dwellings with thatched roofs, as at Auchindrain. Mylne's double church, at the end of the street, of Arran freestone in perfect proportion, came later. It was finished in 1802, and is two churches in one, for Gaelic and English services. The steeple has gone, but money may be found one day to put it back.

What gives most character to the northern approach to Inveraray are the archways unifying the buildings of the waterfront, Mylne's idea and an inspired one since the five arches give a feeling of light and space to the glittering town. Under a sixth arch passes the Dalmally road, the way to Loch Awe.

The road goes over the pass formed by the River Aray, hence the name Inveraray, the town at the mouth of the river. There is a fine impression of the turreted castle half a mile uphill from the arch, where you look through a thin screen of trees to the green parks against a setting of loch backed by the Arrochar Alps.

Road and river take a northward line and separate just a short distance before the top of the pass, the Aray to its westerly source, the road deviating slightly east to pass the big cairn erected to the memory of Neil Munro of Inveraray, journalist, novelist and poet. Now comes the swift descent to the former stronghold of the Campbells before their centre of gravity shifted in 1415 to Inveraray.

Down there at the north-eastern corner of the loch is Kilchurn Castle, built by Sir Colin Campbell in 1440 when the clan expanded out of their original Loch Awe stronghold on Innischonnail. Kilchurn was no more than a square tower at first, the turrets and battlements being added some 250 years later. Looming above the low frost mist of an October morning, against steaming loch and the soaring brown peaks of Cruachan, the castle has a Wagnerian grandeur, haunting and lingering as that music.

Railway and road pass within less than a mile of Kilchurn Castle turning the rivers Orchy and Strae where they combine to enter the Loch, after which they are squeezed under the great wall of Cruachan to make outlet by the Pass of Brander. No one with pretensions to being a mountaineer should miss the chance of climbing at least one of the seven peaks of Cruachan, or better still, take in the two main peaks known as the Taynuilt peak and the Dalmally peak, 3,611 ft and 3,689 ft respectively.

A good quick way up is from the Falls of Cruachan, path-finding through natural oaks and birches to come out on the private road leading to the reservoir. From there it is a simple matter to gain the ridge and traverse the two shapeliest peaks for a unique view of the seaways of Dalriada, with Mull just across the Firth of Lorn and beneath you Loch Awe narrowing like a river to the south-west. The Gaelic meaning 'River Loch' perfectly describes Loch Awe. Observe carefully the mountains: north-west the peaks of Glen Coe, eastwards Ben Lui and the passes leading to Loch Lomond. No wonder the Campbells were a powerful clan on this cross-roads of glens, lochs and sea lochs.

Cruachan in winter is a different proposition, as it was the last time I went to it on a February day of blowing spume and tearing wind. Wrapped up as we were for the sternest conditions, the wind seemed to cut right through us as we hacked steps up the final slope. Forcing ourselves on through the assaulting ice-particles we could have been on Everest, and that was the impression when suddenly in front of us a dazzling wedge solidified before us, vanishing then reappearing in a dazzle of sunshine as the whirling spume and vapour subsided. The wind had suddenly lost half its force.

Clear of the mist the whole ridge lay revealed, transformed to mushrooms of feathery ice. The 'mushrooms' were, of course, half-submerged boulders, and we had to be careful because sometimes a foot plunged through the icy crust into holes between them. Loch Etive and Ben Starav were only dimly visible, as was Loch Awe.

It was too cold to eat in comfort, so we pressed east to Drochaid Glas, enjoying the curling ridge for a mile, still in the sun while most of the world was in gloom. The pink of alpenglow and a curious fragment of blood-red loch warned us it was time to be heading south. Good hard snow at a steep angle led us down swiftly for 1,000 ft, then we were amongst bulges of clear ice, covering rocks and open slopes like a flowing glacier. We picked a way down with infinite care, knowing we would never be able to arrest a fall if we slipped. Back down to the corrie reservoir at dusk it felt almost warm after the arctic conditions above 1,500 ft.

The high reservoir results from impounding the corrie streams behind a dam and pumping water from Loch Awe 1,200 ft into it, using off-peak power from the South of Scotland Electricity Board at night and at weekends. Then when the day-time demand from Cruachan is high, the water from the reservoir can be brought down through the giant underground power station housing four 100 megawatt generators. This pumped storage system set up a height record for the operation of this kind of plant and was a bold project since it was the first of its kind in Scotland.

Loch Awe is the longest loch in Scotland at 25.47 miles, beating Loch Lomond and Loch Ness, its only rivals, though both of these lochs contain more water, for Loch Awe is relatively shallow, less than one-third of its 9,505 acres being over 100 ft deep. Its main peculiarity, however, is that it drains not from its long and narrow southern end but from the Cruachan end, east by the Pass of Brander, so let's go round the loch anticlockwise beginning with the most dramatic scenery.

The transition from broad waters speckled with wooded islands to narrowing loch becoming surging black river is swift. After half-a-dozen miles you are in a canyon walled by rocky gullies. No doubt this is the origin of 'River Loch', from the Gaelic *Abh* which was anglicized to Awe. To learn the topography and appreciate its history and natural history you should stop at Bridge of Awe and climb the south shoulder of the hill to look down on the pass and see the connection between Loch Awe and Loch Etive, separated by less than three miles.

This is where Robert the Bruce subdued the MacDougalls who were holding out against his kingship in 1308. He outwitted John of Lorn from this west side of the pass by showering down arrows on the enemy when they thought they were dealing with only a frontal attack. The supporting Campbells profited, as they did more spectacularly when the rebellious MacDonalds lost their lands to the Campbells in the late fifteenth century. It was then they moved from Loch Awe to Inveraray.

The moving glaciers of the last big advance of ice waged an older battle for the Pass of Brander 12,000 years ago. Their weight was against Cruachan, pressing from the north-east until the ice found a weakness in the western lavas and bulldozed a way towards the glaciers of Loch Etive. So a new outlet to Loch Awe was created, replacing the outlet from the south created by earlier ice ages. Hydroelectric engineers now control the discharging water by tunnelling some of it three miles to empty into Loch Etive through a power station.

To motor down the north side of the loch means turning off at Taynuilt and taking single-track roads through Glen Nant through delightful woods and over a low pass to Kilchrennan. Eastwards of you is the least known part of Loch Awe, yet it is easily explored on farm tracks, and Taychreggan is a good place to stay.

Your eyes will be drawn to the little islands clad in pristine woodland and scrub, with ruins of castles, convents and chapels on them. With a hired boat you could have a rewarding day, landing on Fraoch Eilean and looking at the Norman castle which Bruce took from the MacDougalls and gave to Sir Niall Campbell in 1308 for his loyalty to the crown, and then to Inishail for its burial ground and carved stones. The chapel there is thirteenth century.

Vast spruce plantations stretch ahead blanketing much of the shore and growing high on the hills through Inverinin past the Forestry Commission village of Dalavich. This bit of the loch, formerly inaccessible because of the roughness of its tracks, now supports a fair population of woodsmen, and timber production amounts to something like 100,000 tons a year, mostly for pulp and sawlogs.

Down at Ford we are on a broader road with faster driving up the more open south shore, but speed should be resisted, for the deciduous woods of Ederline Forest and the interesting shore line should be lingered over. The deepest water in the loch is out from Braevallich at over 300 ft showing how down-cutting was the action of earlier glaciers before the cutting of the Pass of Brander removed the pressure. The first of the Campbell strongholds lies just north of Portinnisherrich on the tiny island of Innischonnail close inshore. The ruins of the castle still stand.

The little piers dotting the shore are relics of the time when pleasure steamers plied on the loch, before increasing numbers of motor cars put them out of business. In earlier times, even up to the end of the nineteenth century, travellers between Highlands and Lowlands depended on ferries and private boats across the lochs and sea lochs.

Port Sonachan was an important staging place on the direct route to Inveraray, with a ferry from Taychreggan serving cattle and their drovers coming from the north. Both sides of the loch here have attractive hostelries for fishermen, one of the advantages of Loch Awe being that it is open water, no permits being required for salmon, trout or sea trout.

In terms of West Highland geography it is revealing to consider how early travellers and cattle drovers made their way to the south and east from western Argyll. Earlier on I wrote of Dunadd and the routes by the Leckan Muir to Auchindrain and Loch Fyne. Through these low hills came other traffic, ponies with panniers of charcoal to feed the iron furnace on the shore of the loch south of Auchindrain. The iron-smelting days are remembered by the place name 'Furnace' in an industry that continued from 1754 into the nineteenth century. North of Furnace there was an important ferry crossing to Strachur, used by cattle drovers taking their herds to Dunoon and Ardentinney by the narrow valley containing Loch Eck.

For the Dunbartonshire and Stirlingshire markets the route was to the head of Loch Fyne and continuing north-west by Glen Fyne, to strike east by the Lairig Arnan to reach Glen Falloch near the head of Loch Lomond. A more direct variation of this was to go by Glen Shira from Inveraray into Glen Falloch by the Dubh Eas. Another route to Loch Lomond was by the line taken by the modern road, round the head of Loch Fyne to cross through the hills by the first opening eastward, by Glen Kinglas and over the Arrochar Alps by high Loch Restil descending beneath the Cobbler to the head of Loch Long, then across the short neck of land to Tarbert.

These Arrochar hills offer the finest mountaineering south of Glen Coe, and being within little more than an hour from Glasgow have been documented and guide-booked very thoroughly. The Cobbler is the *pièce de résistance*, three horns of grey rock more difficult in appearance than in actuality, yet only the summit of the North Peak can be reached without rock climbing. If this alone is your objective, then the easiest way is from half way up Glen Croe, striking directly east up one long steep slope.

Much less of a grind because of the variety of the approach is the way up from Loch Long, parking your car at the Naval Torpedo Station. The burn coming down off the mountain here is the Allt á Bhalachain and a path goes up its left side into the corrie. A good landmark is the 'Narnain Stone', offering shelter below its roof. Immediately opposite rise the three prongs of the Cobbler called South, Centre and North Peaks.

The South is the hardest but the way up its left-hand ridge is no more than an easy scramble to rock climbers. More difficult is the way down to the col but men with an eye for a route will notice the leftward-running ledge just below the top, leading to a knobbly cleft with good holds. The upraised arm of the Cobbler himself, Centre Peak, is easier, through the eye of the needle to an exposed ledge for a bold step up on to the highest point.

The North Peak is the only one which is absolutely easy but its bold overhanging face offers the longest and some of the hardest routes in the Arrochar district. From the summit edge you can look down these intimidating walls but such brinkmanship is not for everyone. The more general view is equally exciting, down the length of Loch Long to the Firth of Clyde and the Arran hills, and from Ben Lomond to Cruachan and Ben Nevis.

Beinn an Lochain, 2,992 ft, is the easiest of the Arrochar Alps to climb because the car can be driven to the top of the Rest and be Thankful road, leaving only 2,000 ft of actual climbing to the twin summits. Standing mid-way between Loch Long and Loch Fyne and commanding all the hills of Cowal it is a fine viewpoint for the peaks of the Argyll Forest Park. Three hours is all that is needed for the return trip from the car park. The best way up is to walk a mile west along the Lochgoilhead road before going north up the burn.

Lochgoilhead is an easy spin from here, but a more exciting way to it is through the hills from Ardgartan on Loch Long by the Coilessan Glen over the rugged hills of Argyll's Bowling Green. Among forests, peaks and fjords, you can hardly believe yourself to be so close to Glasgow yet in country where herons nest in holly trees and eagles have their eyries and breed successfully.

This is the wildest bit of the Argyll National Park, yet just across

9 *Climbers on the Cobbler in the rocky world above Loch Long.*
Left, the Gareloch, and in the distance the Firth of Clyde

Loch Long is the Finnart Oil Terminal where giant tankers sail in and oil is pumped across country to Grangemouth. Down there also is the *Polaris* base, with supply ships and nuclear submarines coming and going. The Celtic and Viking seaways have been NATOized.

Where the headlands of Cowal end in the Clyde Estuary we take our leave of it. This is yachtsman's country, more easily accessible from Glasgow than from the north. Frequent car ferries from Gourock make it easy of access for the motorist, and of 'doon the water' resorts Dunoon is the most famous, with Rothesay a good second.

To know it all intimately would take a lifetime.

10   *The sea-lock at Crinan: Campbeltown fishermen lay up their boats for the weekend*

11   *Forestry workers knock off work in Glen Branter. Sawn logs will go to the pulp mill at Fort William*

CHAPTER THREE

Loch Lomond and Glen Coe

Loch Lomond—Rannoch Moor—Glen Coe

When the Vikings launched their raiding ships in Loch Lomond before the Battle of Largs, they did so by sailing up Loch Long from the Clyde, landing at Arrochar and hauling their longships overland to Tarbert. The leader of the expedition was King Magnus of Man, and he knew his geography: that by sailing down through the inhabited islands he could get back into the Clyde by the Leven, past Dumbarton Castle. So while King Hakon waited to do battle with Alexander III, his son-in-law Magnus was murdering and pillaging the Lennox. The Scots were shortly to extract retribution as force of arms defeated the enemy on land and storms of sudden violence broke up their fleet. By this victory the Vikings were pushed back from the West to the Orkneys and Shetlands, never again to bother the West.

Loch Lomond is the gateway to the Western Highlands, with its great pyramid of a Ben dominating the Lowlands, bulky-looking even from Glasgow on clear days. The public road up the eastern side ends below it, at Rowardennan. Up the western side runs the A82, the main road, fast enough to Luss and from then on snaking round the twisting shore for half its 22 miles—yes, a headache and a source of congestion and frustration in the caravan season. Yet it is a journey of which I never tire, even if I am on the way to more distant places like Loch Awe or Glen Coe.

Loch Lomond is where I have chosen to make my home, at Gartocharn on the southern shore fairly close to the Nature Reserve, where the River Endrick winds to a marshy mouth often flooded in winter, and in spring filled with the sounds of the Hebrides when the wading birds return, redshanks, curlews, oyster catchers, ringed plovers, dunlin, lapwings and passing whimbrel and greenshank. Terns, sheld duck, shoveller, mallard and teal flight continually, while in the tall trees the herons fly in and out of their big nests on top of the trees. Ospreys are not infrequent visitors. I have had one bank swiftly and splash down within fifty yards of me, rising with a pike slung from one talon. For weeks on end a goshawk and a hen harrier occupied the Gartocharn bog, sparring continually, to the delight of innumerable bird watchers attracted by the good news.

Loch Lomond is unique amongst Scottish lochs for the variety of its wild life and scenery, perhaps best appreciated from this south-eastern shore by taking a short walk to the little knoll above Balmaha pier. Stand there and you are on the Highland Boundary Fault, looking down on the island of Inchcailloch 200 yards across the water. Follow its wooded spine to the west shore, then swing your head 180 degrees to the top of Conic Hill just above you. That fault runs right across Scotland to Stonehaven, dividing Highlands and Lowlands.

Nowhere is it so dramatically seen as here, however, where the broad waters lapping green shores and low hills suddenly become hemmed in by tawny mountain walls and the loch becomes a narrowing trench biting north through oak-wooded shores. Of the twelve large islands dotting the five-miles-broad southern loch only two are farmed today. One of them, Inchfad, lies very close, just north of Inchcailloch, so their contrasts can be taken at a glance.

Inchfad has been largely cleared to make fields and clearly exhibits the influence of man. Inchcailloch by comparison is densely wooded in oaks of almost pristine naturalness with an under flora of very great interest to the scientific botanist. Torrinch and Creinch and Clairinch lie close to Inchcailloch and all four form part of the Loch Lomond Nature Reserve.

The Nature Conservancy invite you to land on Inchcailloch and learn about the island from their pamphlet. You pick one up as you land and learn as you follow their well-laid-out nature trail to a fine viewpoint on top. *Cailloch* is the Gaelic for 'old woman', and the island takes its name from the nuns of AD 717 who came here following the death of St Kentigern. Good archaeological work has been done here of recent years to lay bare the ruins of a twelfth-century church. It would have been in use when Robert the Bruce came hunting here in 1326 and it continued to be used for hundreds of years afterwards. Note the tombstone of Gregor MacGregor, grandfather of Rob Roy.

Just below Inchcailloch, and at Strathcashel Point to the north, are the remnants of crannogs—lake dwellings. Built up on sunken rocks they were artificial islands built for security, no doubt. They might even have been in use when the Viking raiders came pillaging down the loch. Traces of ancient furrows and ruins on other islands show that most were farmed in these ancient times. Fallow deer are the most frequent users of the islands today, swimming from one to the other. Introduced for royal sport, probably before the time of Bruce, they maintain their numbers at between 70 and 90.

The driving road from Balmaha to Rowardennan has to be taken carefully, as it winds and climbs past a succession of little bays beloved of caravanners. Glasgow University have a research station about two miles from Rowardennan and over a long period of years have built up a great body of knowledge of the fish life, which is greater in variety than in any other Scottish loch.

When I visited Dr Harry Slack, who is in charge of the station, I was lucky to be shown some newly caught powan, a good pike and a lovely perch. The catch was the result of three hours' netting in the catamaran, which is fitted with echo-sounding gear and electrical equipment for hydrographic work. 'The powan are the most plentiful fish in the loch, and I think the perch next,' he explained.

Handling some of them, he showed me lamprey scars which had healed. The lampreys have the unpleasant habit of attaching themselves by suction to any fish to obtain a meal of flesh and blood. Powan feed mainly on plankton so are not normally taken by rod and line. But what is a powan? Dr Slack calls them ice-age freshwater white-fish, but the local name is freshwater herring.

It is a sea fish which in the beginning came to fresh water only to spawn. The theory is that it had to adapt to a permanent habitat of salt-free water when the land rose slightly at the end of the glacial period, cutting the fish off from its migration streams. An indication of its ice-age origin is that it requires Loch Lomond to be at its coldest in early January before it can spawn and hatch its eggs in late March.

We discussed the theory that Loch Lomond was a relatively small loch among the mountains, when the powan was impounded in what may have been gravelly water and decaying ice lobes. The Forth then occupied what is now the broad southern basin of Loch Lomond in these days more than 10,000 years ago. The modern loch dates from the land lifting as the weight of the ice melted.

Before that time, maybe by a few thousand years, there was only solid mountain with rivers running down to the Forth from what was a plateau formation. The hollow occupied by Loch Lomond was carved out by a re-advance of ice. Glen Luss and the River Endrick, originally one east-flowing stream, were severed by the cutting action of ice. The same holds good for Inveruglas and Inversnaid waters. They were one stream until ice bulldozed a 600-ft trench. The deepest part of the loch now lies between the streams.

Flounders are known to make their way up the 22 miles of the loch though the deep waters to its very head, where they have been taken by Dr Slack at 80 ft. A 47-lb pike has been caught on Loch Lomond. Other fish which occur in the loch are salmon, trout, seatrout, minnow, perch, loach, eel, three-spined stickleback, ten-spined stickleback, roach, lampern, sea lamprey and brook lamprey. Fishing permits can be had at Rowardennan Hotel at 50 pence per day.

Rowardennan is the starting point for the easiest way up Ben Lomond by a path which begins just opposite the hotel, leading in four miles to the summit. The best of it is the final pyramid with the plunge of the north face below and the islands spread on the broad triangle of loch seeming to edge the Clyde. Now you can look down on the whole Viking route, with Tarbert just below you and Loch Long opening just beyond the narrow neck of land separating fresh water from salt. Clearly they had a better sense of topography than most people have today, for the relationship of Loch Lomond to the Clyde is not generally understood.

Look the other way eastward and you can see Loch Katrine. Remember that I described in the last chapter how the drovers took their cattle through the hills from Loch Fyne to the head of Loch Lomond. One of the ways from there to the Stirlingshire market was through Glen Gyle to Loch Katrine and over the hills to Aberfoyle, then by Flanders Moss to the Carron Valley and Falkirk. Some of these cattle would have come from Jura and Islay, spending a week to ten days on the road.

This is Rob Roy country and even today Craig Rostan is a wild place, cleft by the great ravine of the Cailness Burn just beyond the north shoulder of Ben Lomond. Using the paddle-steamer *Maid of the Loch* on a Saturday or Sunday you can snatch a wonderful walk on six miles of track between morning and afternoon calls at the piers. Stepping off the morning boat at Inversnaid you have five hours before it leaves from Rowardennan.

The north-to-south traverse is the best way to do it, beginning at the footbridge which spans the Inversnaid waterfall and following the path through oaks forming a roof over your head. No bother finding the way as it contours the steep banks, blue and yellow with wild hyacinths and primroses in the spring. May is the perfect time, when the trees are loud with stuttering wood warblers and the jangling notes of redstarts. The sharp-eyed visitor may even see a pied fly-catcher.

Above you the mountain rises in rocky steps, where red deer, wild goats, buzzard and eagle come as no surprise. You enjoy your peace all the more for the constant procession of cars streaming up the other side of the loch under the big pipes of the Loch Sloy power station. Nothing impinges here. The path passes ruins of former crofts, with one inhabited house just ahead at Cailness. The fibreglass boat with outboard engine is the shepherd's link with the outside world at Tarbet, where he collects his mail and groceries. But this happy naturalist-cum-shepherd never wants to leave. He finds fulfilment here.

Past the big gorge you are inside the boundary of the Queen Elizabeth Forest Park and all too soon you join a bulldozed track which leads back to Rowardennan. Alas, however, these peaceful days may be coming to an end, for at the time of writing (1972) surveyors are busy calculating the feasibility of building a reservoir high on Ben Lomond's north-western shoulder, so that water could be pumped into it from the loch to be brought down through generators as required. The scheme would be similar to the one on Cruachan. It is my hope that it won't prove to be feasible, and Loch Sloy across the loch will be the focus for future hydro-electric plans.

A stand must be taken by the public to preserve the beauties of Loch Lomond, especially when it is within such easy reach of three-quarters of the population of Scotland. True, it had to become a reservoir in 1971 due to the chronic shortage of water in the central belt, but the conversion was done with sensitive regard to loch levels so that the little bays and semi-aquatic vegetation would not be lost by inundation.

The control is done by a barrage on the River Leven aiming at a level of 26 ft OD. In practice the loch fluctuates very considerably rising to 30 ft above Ordnance Datum in flood and in drought falling to as low a level as 23 ft. From the Ross Priory Pumping Station below Gartocharn the loch sends out 100,000,000 gallons daily to Renfrew, Dumbarton, Kirkintilloch, Stirling, Falkirk and West Lothian. The lochside part of the scheme is most inconspicuous.

The barrage is at Balloch, terminus of the electric trains which leave Glasgow Queen Street for Loch Lomond every half-hour—a journey of under 50 minutes. Departure point for the steamer, Balloch, should be a beautiful place, but it is an eyesore and an affront to town and country planners. Studies have been done, imaginative plans drawn up, but no step forward has been taken since 1949 when Sir Patrick Abercrombie published his weighty *Clyde Valley Regional Plan* showing this as the perfect site for a National Recreation Centre.

There is little inducement to stop in Balloch but there is plenty at Duck Bay, only two miles on, as the first wide vista of the loch opens up and a loop road invites you to picnic. Here you are looking across the greatest breadth of the loch, peppered with islands, and dominated by the most massive aspect of Ben Lomond seen in its entirety with blunt head rising squarely from broad shoulders.

The shortest distance between shores here is five miles of easily ruffled water, for this 'fault basin' is shallow where the glacier was able to fan out on meeting the softer rocks. The islands are no more than gritty masses standing above a 50-ft depth of water. The depth increases as the loch narrows, reaching a maximum in the Tarbet basin at 600 ft.

Duck Bay offers the delights of a marina, ice-cream vans, a stately youth hostel, and just across the water on Inchmurrin, a water-skiing centre and hotel. On that island nearest the shore the Earls of Lennox had their stronghold. The fourteenth-century castle is a ruin now, and until the early years of this century the island was maintained as a fallow deer park.

Motoring north, on the fastest bit of the Loch Lomond road, you pass the stronghold of the Colquhouns, whose chief still sits at Rossdhu.

Look out for the house, seen across a little bay where the road touches the shore. The word conservation is popular today, but no landowners in Scotland have done more in this field than the Colquhouns. Give a thought to them as you twist round the delightful way to Luss, the showpiece village of the loch.

It lies at the foot of a glen, backed by an elegant horseshoe of grassy hills, superb for ski-touring in winter. In front is spattered the main mass of Loch Lomond islands, and to cruise through their narrows in a sailing dinghy reveals how they shelter each other. One moment you are becalmed, then from somewhere comes a puff of wind as you zig-zag through ravine-like narrows such as that between Inchmoan and Inchcruin, where the waterway is only 20 yards.

Inchlonaig is the most northerly of that group, an island of yew trees planted by Robert the Bruce to provide bows for his archers, it is said. It was also a deer-hunting island of the Colquhouns. You can find a lot of peace here, and if you know where to look you may flush capercaillie from the trees, for there is a nesting colony of these greatest of game birds on one of the islands.

North of Inverbeg you are into the country of the MacFarlanes, whose war cry was 'Loch Sloy'! You need your eye on the road for every yard that stretches ahead now on the long haul to the top of the loch. The best plan is to pull into a lay-by when you want to look at the scenery. Better still get out and climb above the road and enjoy the peace.

Inveruglas and its power house lies only four miles on. By asking for a permit here you are allowed to drive up the high climbing road to the big dam impounding Loch Sloy in the heart of the Arrochar Alps. It is a wild rocky place between the 3,000-ft peaks of Ben Vorlich and Ben Vane. A branch road slightly lower down opens up two more peaks, Ben Narnain and Ben Ime—highest in the range. Motoring back down the Inveruglas Water you should take account of the Inversnaid waterfall on the other side of the loch, remembering that these two streams were once one before the glaciers dredged them apart.

The loch gradually shallows out now from 400 to 200 ft in the next few miles. Note the castles perched on the tiny Inveruglas Isle and Island I Vow. Look out for the Pulpit Rock by the roadside just north of the latter island, cut out at the beginning of the nineteenth century to serve as a church until one was built at Ardlui at the head of the loch, where the River Falloch enters.

At Inverarnain, and a mile on at an awkward little bridge, you will see the big glens which the drovers used to reach from the west. A mile past that little bridge, to the north west of the railway, there is a famous group of great stones. The name for them is *Clach nam Breatann*, 'Stone of the Britons', believed to mark the northern boundary of the British kingdom of Strathclyde whose capital was Dumbarton, and which they had to defend against the Picts and later the Scots from Dalriada. The kingdom lasted until 1043, with Dumbarton as gateway to the Western Isles.

The most difficult walk on Loch Lomondside is from Glen Falloch to Inversnaid leaving the road below the great waterfall at Benglas Farm. The route is not difficult at first through a little pass in the hills to the shore past two ruined crofts. The difficulties begin after that as you are pushed up a jungly hillside, much broken by gullies. There is a path of sorts if you keep high enough, which drops down eventually to pass Rob Roy's cave on the shore below. The cave can more easily be visited from Inversnaid by walking northward for a mile along a good footpath, then at a big crag descending broken and rather slippery rock to the hole amongst the boulders, where Rob and his men met to carry out cattle-thieving raids.

The famous outlaw had acquired a wonderful topographical knowledge of Loch Lomond and all its approaches, having lived in Glen Shira to the west and Glen Gyle to the east before settling at Craig Rostan. Thorn in the flesh as he was, you have to admire his boldness, emerging from his lair to swoop down on the barracks near Inversnaid, built in 1713 for the troops who were trying to subdue him. It is a tribute to his cunning that he died quietly in his cottage in 1738. He is buried in Balquidder churchyard and his ghost might have permitted itself a wry smile when vandals robbed the grave of its copper chains and fixtures in 1970. I can even see a nod of approval, when useless fixtures could be lifted to earn good money.

It was because of men like Rob Roy that cattle-drovers were allowed a gun, sword and pistol, to defend themselves, even although the disarming acts of 1716 and 1748 made carrying of arms illegal. Drovers were allowed to carry weapons even during the '45 once their loyalty to the Crown had been ascertained, which shows the importance of the cattle trade to a Britain always short of meat.

Now we drive north to Glen Coe by following the road climbing from the head of the Loch Lomond by Glen Falloch to Crianlarich and the junction between east and west. Shapely peaks stand round you here, all more than 3,000 ft, the highest Ben More and Stobinian at over 3,800 ft. None are difficult, but good climbers have died here in winter by simple slips, when the slopes were frozen. In the main, however, these hills are among the safest to learn snow and ice climbing. Distances are short and ridges linking the peaks are high and exhilarating.

The north road goes along Strath Fillan to Tyndrum, passing the old Caledonian wood of Coninish. The spade-shaped peak at the head of this glen is Ben Lui (3,708 ft) famous for its alpine plants and north-eastern corrie where the Tay rises. The direct way up that spade shape in winter is one of the classics of Scottish mountaineering and may involve over 1,000 ft of step-cutting, finishing on a vertical or perhaps over-hanging snow cornice. The base of the corrie in mid-summer is a natural rock garden of roseroot and saxifrages of several kinds.

Next to Ben Lui is Ben Dubhchraig, best approached from the bridge where the Tyndrum road crosses the river. This makes a fine ski trip in early winters, when the pine woods are powdered and the approach march becomes a delight. You need sealskins over the soles of your skis in such conditions, to prevent the skis slipping backwards as you climb. Higher up the snow will probably be wind-packed, maybe ridged into furrows, but basically easy for fast turning. The run down will well repay the two or three hours labour of ascent and when road conditions are difficult it makes a good alternative to Glen Coe.

Tyndrum is an important junction, with two railways and two roads going in different directions, west to Oban and north to Bridge of Orchy. Glen Coe lies north over a pass from Perthshire into Argyllshire with a thrilling view of new mountains, the shapely cone of Ben Dorain to the right. Leftward the jostling summits of the Black Mount, and in the centre Meall a' Bhuridh dominating the brown mat of Rannoch Moor. It can only be fully appreciated when the high tops are covered in snow.

Bridge of Orchy is a great division. The railway is forced away eastward. The road forges ahead, past Loch Tulla, pine trees and shapely grouping of exciting peaks. Don't drive too fast on that straight road or you will miss the sight of deer, the ringing cry of greenshank or the sight of golden eagles, perhaps even an osprey. I'll deal more fully with the country lying west of Loch Tulla in the chapter on Oban and Loch Etive.

Now you begin climbing the great loop of the Black Mount to that strange plateau of peaty lochs, moss and boulders, which is Rannoch Moor. On your left is the enormous horseshoe of Coire Ba, the biggest corrie in Scotland, scooped from Clachlet and Stob Ghabhair, peaks which emphasize the loneliness of the empty eastward sweep of the moor on your right. You are far to the west here, yet all the drainage of the streams is eastward, to the Tay, by Loch Rannoch and Loch Tummel.

Canoeists can have fun, linking the lochs trailing across it by Loch Ba and Loch Laidon, roughly ten miles of wriggling waterway with little islands and sandy bays to enliven the scene. The moor is no dull place, but alive with birds in spring and summer. Nor is walking difficult in dry weather if you watch where you are going, keeping clear of the spongier sections.

Yet it is in these wet sections you will find the nesting dunlin and golden plover, perhaps even find that rare plant *Scheuchzeria palustris*, the Rannoch rush which grows nowhere else in Scotland but here. The roots everywhere in the bogs tell of the vanished pine forest which once covered this moor, giving shelter to brown bears, caribou, northern lynx, great elk, beaver and wolf. Foresters have started to put back the trees on Rannoch Moor, mainly at the Gorton south-eastern section of the moor. Experimental plots have also been planted by the roadside north of Loch Ba and seem to be doing well. Most people, however, prefer Rannoch Moor the bleak way it is and hope it will never become just another conifer blanket.

For those who want only a quick look at the moor the chair-lift on Meall a' Bhuridh offers an immediate panoramic view of the watery tableland which was once a mighty reservoir of ice spilling north-eastwards into the Spey valley and south-westwards beyond Loch Tulla. The chair-lift was built to exploit the skiing potential of this most sporting mountain in the West Highlands, on a north face which holds snow from December into late May in most years. A drag lift goes almost to the summit at 3,636 ft.

Unfortunately it can be a savage place for weather, sunless till February and too often windy and wet. You marvel at your enthusiasm when you go up there in whiteout and ski down Happy Valley by instinct rather than vision. But you find yourself enjoying it and go back for more. Real rewards come, however: keen frosts after falls of powder snow, sparkling sun and windless air. Then you can discover what a mountain this is, poised above the wrinkled mat of the eiderdown moor and facing across to Ben Nevis.

The standard of skiing is extremely high, mostly among working-class enthusiasts who buy season tickets and never miss a weekend, come hail, hurricane or blizzard. You get to know nearly everybody using the upper slopes, for it is no place for beginners. The nursery area is by the plateau, with a handy little tow to take the strain out of climbing. Given a good day and not too many people on the hill, you can do 15,000 ft of downhill running easily in half-a-dozen hours, but you have to be fit.

Meall a' Bhuridh is in fact the first peak of the Glen Coe Boundary Fault, but it is announced more dramatically across Glen Etive on Buachaille Etive Mor, three miles away. Motoring towards it, you watch it change its shape from a blunt wall of rock to a sculptured rock point, supported by pink ribs and flying buttresses. The tower which stands out from the summit is the top of the Crowberry Ridge, Scotland's most famous rock climb. On that mountain there is something for everybody, the hardest of hard gully and wall climbs, easy buttresses or the hardest of severities. Many of the happiest days of my life in summer and winter have been spent on that mountain and others in Glen Coe.

But rather than rhapsodize, I should like to tell you something about its geology, for you cannot separate mountain scenery and geology, since one is the consequence of the other. The porphyritic lavas of these mountains resulted from their welling up and subsiding into a cauldron of granite magma, hence the term 'cauldron subsidence' for the nine miles by five miles which constitutes Glen Coe.

So let's go on to the Buachaille Etive Mor. The easiest way is from Coire na Tulaich above the little white-washed cottage of Laggan-garbh, the climbers' hut. No rock climbing is involved: nothing harder than steep scree at the top of the corrie, then an easy slant up the summit ridge. Following the high crest over all its tops, you get a grasp of the main topography of the cauldron.

You notice that the bulky peaks stretching west of you are aligned parallel to your own, stretching back south-westwards from bold rocky fronts. Buachaille Etive Beag matches Buachaille Etive Mor, and behind it is Ben Fhada with Bidian nam Bian (3,766 ft) rising beyond and throwing a spur eastward over Stob Coire nam Lochan (3,657 ft) to Aonach Dubh. It is the mass of ridges that makes route finding in this massif so complex in misty weather. And because of the steepness of the approach slopes the Bidian in snow has a reputation second only to Ben Nevis as a killer mountain.

The difficulty is that it is all too easy to take the wrong ridge and find yourself on steepening ground becoming cliffs. Map reading and compass work must be exact if you are to find your way round the nine tops and three precipitous corries of the Bidian massif. On these tops, which go to 3,600 ft, you will find granite boulders that have been lifted from Rannoch Moor and carried over the summits by ice-age glaciers. Conversely, the ice moved in the opposite direction in the last big advance, when Glen Coe's rocks were transported to Rannoch Moor by the valley of the River Ba.

To explore Bidian you motor across the watershed past 'the gorge' and park near the National Trust signpost pointing the 'Meeting of the Three Waters'. The mountains have drawn together now, walling the pass. The black noses of rock protruding on the south are the Three Sisters, and between the first two hangs a ravine called the 'Lost Valley'. The path climbing up its torrent is the way to the Bidian if you would have the most scenic approach.

Down to the footbridge and up the right hand side is the obvious way, but higher up, where a hanging jungle of birches and boulders compress the ravine, you have to find your own way, fording the torrent as best you can to a scree slope on the other side where walking is easier. In autumn when the rowans flame against the dark rocks this is the most colourful place in Glen Coe.

Then suddenly you emerge on to a flat that was once the site of a lochan, a heart-lifting place open to the peaks. There is a great boulder but no mountain stream. The torrent you followed has vanished. It flows underground. Walk ahead and you pick it up again, draining down between Bidian nam Bian and Beinn Fhada.

You can either go straight ahead to the col between the two peaks mentioned or you can keep with the stream and curve rightward to the col separating Stob Coire nam Lochan and Bidian nam Bian. It is then an easy matter to take in these peaks connected to each other by a narrow ridge. Superb views open up: down Loch Etive on one side and out to the Hebrides, or across the north ridge of Glen Coe to Ben Nevis. The rock here is andesite, and a good traverse from the summits is to follow the west ridge from Stob Coire nam Beith towards An t-Sron and strike down the first col north-eastwards into the north-north-west corrie.

For a corrie containing so much verticality the walking is remarkably easy. You are in fact on the extremity of the Glen Coe Fault Intrusion where the porphyrite merges into granite. The large outcrops of fine-grained, pink-and-grey granitoid rock indicate where the granite magma rose as the plug of porphyritic lavas subsided. You can see it on Meall Dearg of Aonach Eagach, whose long frontage forms the north retaining wall of Glen Coe.

The traverse of that north ridge is the best high-level scramble in Glen Coe. The usual way of doing it is from the eastern end at 900 ft, before the road plunges down to Clachaig. Am Bodach (3,085 ft) lies immediately above: a straight-forward grind to the delights of the narrowing ridge with its little rock steps and airy pinnacles—nothing difficult but not for the nervous. Wise climbers will not try to leave the ridge and strike directly down to Glen Coe, for the gullies are unpleasantly rotten and the rock is loose. Many incautious scramblers have been benighted trying short-cuts. The easy way down is from Sgor nam Fiannaidh with a straight-forward descent down grass slopes. The best line down is just east of the summit.

Even if only the simplest top of Aonach Eagach is gained, it is worthwhile for the contrasts between the opposing walls of Glen Coe. The north side sweeps down to the valley floor unbreached by any corrie, whereas on the other side the peaks have been gouged by deep-cut valleys ending in wild amphitheatres of corries whose openings are kept by The Sisters on sinister guard.

Much of the austerity of Glen Coe comes from the effect of Atlantic weather upon its topography of rock spurs, hidden glens where the mist boils and the dramatic disclosures of impossibly high peaks are glimpsed through openings in the clouds. And that weather affects the climber very seriously, making demands on his judgement, his physique, his confidence and his skill. Climb safely on the crags and ridges of Glen Coe in all seasons of the year and you will have demonstrated a certain ability to survive.

Of dozens of weekends spent in Glen Coe I must tell my strangest experience, on a February night, when two of us tramped up Glen Leac na Muic in the rainy darkness hoping we would be able to find a barn and not have to pitch the tent. Rob reckoned he knew a place, and sure enough, round a bend in the path we saw the glimmer of light from a shepherd's cottage, the only one in the glen.

'Ay, take the barn, but don't set it on fire,' said the shepherd, 'but what you want climbing hills in this weather beats me. It's thick with snow up there.' The voice was gloomy and pessimistic, but not unfriendly. The barn was a snug place full of hay, about a hundred yards from the house, and we were soon settled inside our sleeping bags, listening the the wind moaning outside—glad indeed we were not camping.

Somewhere in the middle of the night I awoke with Rob shining his torch in my face, in a considerable state of excitement.

'There was a man at that door a moment ago,' he said, 'with a face like clay. He was standing there, but he didn't speak, and when I shone my torch he disappeared.'

'How could you see a face like clay in pitch darkness?' I asked. 'Don't be daft. You've been dreaming. Go to sleep.'

'I'm telling you, Tom, he was there. A man with a face that had no blood in it, but there was blood on his clothes. The eyes were like sunk-in holes. It wasn't a dream. I'm sure of it.'

And to my surprise he was still talking about it next day as we climbed Sgur na h-Ulaidh on a foul day of driving snow, made suddenly worthwhile when, on the summit, there was a rent torn in the enveloping clouds and we looked for an instant on a vast array of snow-covered mountain tops plunging into glens of impenetrable depth.

Then the black slashes of sea lochs and ocean were swallowed up again in the turmoil of storm, and we had to fight our way off the mountain, heads down to the storm. It was late afternoon before we got back to the barn and were in the act of stripping off our iced clothing and frozen socks in preparation for a meal when the shepherd appeared.

'You had better come down to the house and sit at the fire,' he said. 'It's too cold here to be cooking, and yourselves half-frozen.' We were only too pleased, and were soon warming up at his fireplace.

The shepherd was a man of few words. 'How did you sleep in the hay?' he asked. I said, jocularly, that my friend had been seeing a ghost, and told the story of the appearance at the door of the man with the face like clay.

He did not laugh. Instead he gave me a penetrating look. 'Well,' he said, 'you know what happened at this spot?'

'To do with the Massacre?' we both asked.

'Yes, to do with the Massacre. It was on the spot where the barn stands that MacIain, the chief of the Clan MacDonald, was murdered, and I am thinking that the man with the face like clay you saw was the ghost of the chief, for this is the anniversary of it.' I felt less sure now that Rob had wholly imagined it.

The story of the infamous massacre has been written too often to tell in detail here. The main scene of the killing was nearer the mouth of the glen, where it becomes open and green as it nears the sea. Around it were scattered the clan in ten settlements when Argyll's regiment with Campbell of Glen Lyon at the head arrived on 1 February looking for billets. The MacDonalds gave them readily enough, when they were assured that the soldiers came in peace.

To accept hospitality and commit murder in the name of the Crown was outside the scope of Highland experience in 1692. The early hours of 13 February of that year was to open a new chapter in treachery, when in darkness the soldiers began chopping down their hosts. We had slept where MacIain was shot in the back. His wife fared worse as the troops tore her clothing from her and used their teeth to force off the rings on her fingers. She died more slowly. And slow death of exposure killed many people who escaped to the hills. Yet most of the 500-strong clan survived, thanks to the very severity of the weather, which delayed a force of 400 troops marching by the Devil's Staircase to cut off the escaping Macdonalds.

One wonders how Campbell of Glen Lyon felt, as he played cards with his hosts after being wined and dined, when he was handed a message which read:

You are hereby ordered to fall upon the rebells the Macdonalds

12   From Buachaille Etive Mor. Clouds fill the hollows of Rannoch Moor like a return of the glaciers

of Glenco and put all to the sword under 70. You are to have special care that the old fox and his sons do not escape your hand. You are to secure all avenues that no man escape. This you are to put into execution at five of the clock precisely. . . . See that this is put into execution with fear or favour or you may expect to be dealt with as one not true to King or Government nor a man fit to carry a Commission in the King's service. Expecting you will not fail in the fulfilling hereof as you love yourself.

Campbell, when called to account, could only show 38 bodies. And he so needed evidence that he even exhibited a baby's hand. The chief's sons were away over the hills with everyone who could walk or be carried; only the fittest survived. They were allowed to return and rebuild their homes the following year, and the clan fought for the Stewarts in 1715 and 1745.

The first MacIain of Glen Coe was the son of Angus Og, Lord of the Isles. The stability of the Highlands was shattered when James IV in 1493 broke their power but created a vacuum without law or order. The clan chiefs had a new freedom of rule resulting in constant feuding and rebellions. The MacDonalds of Glen Coe were adventurous fighters and cattle raiders. When they fought for the great Montrose they solved their victualling problem by lifting beasts from the Campbells. They were at Killiecrankie in 1689 and made their way home via Glen Lyon to scatter the Campbells and lift their cattle as they went.

The excuse for the massacre was MacIain's failure to take the oath of allegiance before a sheriff or depute by 1 January 1692. Exiled King James had advised MacIain to take it. The chief went to Col. Hill at Fort William but was sent on to Inveraray to Campbell of Ardkinglas. The Sheriff was away and the oath was not taken until the 6th.

But King William, to whom he was offering oath, had already decided that 'it will be a proper vindication of public justice to extirpate that sect of thieves'. The Campbells were chosen because it was felt that they would allow no sentiment to interfere with the foul deed.

13   *Skiing down 'Happy Valley' of Meall áBhuridh in Glen Coe.*
       On the left is Buachaille Etive Mor, and Ben Nevis dominates the
       background

14   *Loch Lomond from the Highland Boundary Fault at Balmaha:*
       Looking over Inchfad to Luss

CHAPTER FOUR

Oban, Appin, Mull and Iona

Appin and Benderloch—Loch Tulla to Loch Etive—Oban—Iona and Mull

Emerging from Glen Coe you are on the seaside, on Loch Leven, with the west road running past the narrows of Ballachulish to the open mouth of the wider strait of Loch Linnhe. The south road swings down the Appin coast, loops round Loch Creran and continues along the Benderloch coast to cross Loch Etive at the Falls of Lora. Oban lies just round the corner, with Mull and Iona across the water. The mildness of this sea coast is best appreciated in winter, when the big peaks forming the wild hinterland are white yet every bend of this indented coast brings fresh colours into view.

I remember such a day in February when I set off from Loch Lomondside to ski in Glen Coe, but at Tyndrum was worried by the sudden change from black ice to frozen snow ruts, thinly covered in powder snow. The sliding and bumping was a driver's nightmare, rewarding only for the arctic landscape dazzling in the sunshine. Alas, I had a shock coming to me when, arriving beneath Meall a' Bhuridh, I discovered I had forgotten my ski boots.

In the circumstance I decided to push down the glen and go round the coast to Connel in order to miss another rutted crossing of Rannoch Moor. Motoring through the lower glen, I had to stop now and then to marvel at the savagery of the scene of pendulous ice-falls hanging on the crags and snow powder submerging the peaks. Yet at the seashore was quite a different world, with curlews and oyster catchers piping and a raft of wigeon feeding among some red-breasted mergansers.

The bays were calm and at Portnacroish I had to stop to enjoy the sight of Castle Stalker, like a square rock against a maze of low headlands formed by Lismore and the Lynne of Lorn. Strangely, however, there was a sprinkling of snow round Loch Creran where the hills rise abruptly to 3,000 ft. A high hill-pass leads into Glen Coe from here, used, no doubt, as an escape on that morning of the massacre. Across Loch Etive I was back to dry road again and lemon-tinted grasses beneath pink-tinged snowpeaks. But there was more snow and ice to deal with between Dalmally and Tyndrum before I won through.

Look at that circuit on the map and you will notice that there are no interconnecting roads across that wild hinterland. There is an outstanding cross-country walk from Loch Tulla, however, from the old driving inn of Inveroran west to lonely Loch Dochard ringed by shapely peaks, then by a low pass into Glen Kinglass and Loch Etiveside.

A good time to do it is in the late autumn when the red deer stags are roaring in the corries and all the muted yellows and browns of the rocky slopes seem to echo the wild mystery of the hills. The walk takes you in a twenty-mile loop round the back of Ben Cruachan to a point opposite Bonawe within a short distance of Taynuilt and the main road and rail link to Oban. Motorists should certainly not speed through Taynuilt, but take the little branch road which leads down to a unique industrial monument, a 'bloomery'—an iron furnace —the last to burn native deciduous woods to smelt iron from imported ore in direct contravention of the laws relating to Scotland.

Built in 1753, the well-preserved bloomery operated for the next 120 years, swallowing up the forest of every hillside within range. Ironically the Ministry of Works had to step in to save the building from the octopus arms of invading trees squeezing roots between the stones. The bricks of the chimney have a Welsh trade mark, showing that there could have been no kilns in Scotland when this furnace was built, so they had been imported from Wales.

Four years before the Ministry of Works took action I had reported to the Chief Planner for Scotland that an important link with Scotland's history would be lost if no action was taken to save this old furnace. On that early visit I had talked to a number of old people who could remember stories told to them by the last generation who worked the furnace.

Duncan McLean was one of them. The last of three tenants still living in the 'furnace houses', he could tell me most of the things I wanted to know. 'The furnace was before my time,' he said with a grin, 'but when they were ready to tap the iron they used to ring a bell. I know a man who could remember listening for it. Then he would run up and see the molten metal pouring out of the furnace mouth.'

He took me to the spot. 'You can see the pig-beds. And if you look inside the furnace you will see a bit of iron sticking up inside from the last 'run'. It must have cooled. See how red it is. And look all round you here. It's one big clinker dump of ore with the iron melted out of it.

'Come round the back here and we'll climb up to the sheds where the ore and charcoal were stored. You see how the furnace is in two stories? The reason for that is that the charcoal and iron ore were poured into the closed furnace from above, then a set of bellows below would blow the furnace to the heat required to melt the iron from the slag.'

He showed me where the big iron wheel used to be, turned by water running along a lade from the Rive Awe to power the bellows. Duncan McLean had spent most of his life in the Bonawe quarry across the loch, working 10 hours a day for 1s 1d (5p) an hour, the rate being reduced to 6d (2½p) a ton when the men were laid off to shovel the granite into boats which would sail it down the Falls of Lora for the coastal journey to Glasgow. In the tram-car era it was the Bonawe setts which paved the streets. Today Bonawe quarry is still exporting granite for road building, some of it to the islands.

The quarry life sounded hard, but according to Mrs Bell and Mrs Macintyre it was infinitely better than the furnace. 'I've heard all about it as a girl,' said old Mrs Bell with feeling. 'You were little better than a slave. This house of mine used to be the furnace stores, where the meal and flour was kept. The furnacemen got it on the truck system, at reduced rates. But you were always in debt. Your house, your food and yourself belonged to the furnace, and they would take your cow and brand it 'LF' if you couldn't pay.'

And Mrs Macintyre could tell me that with the coming and going of boats with ore and pig-iron, Taynuilt was a great place for liquor smuggling, so there was no want of a dram. 'Everything here sprang up because of the furnace,' she said. 'The school, the cottages, a church and Kelly's pier down there.'

Who was Kelly? None other than the manager of the furnace, a dark figure responsible to the Newland Company of Coniston, who promoted the industry until long after this wasteful method of smelting iron had been outmoded. In economic terms it took only two tons of coal to smelt one ton of pig-iron at Dixon's in Glasgow, while at Bonawe five tons of timber were required for each ton of pig-iron. But the demand for iron was high, due to the advancing industrial revolution and as long as the timber lasted iron was produced at Loch Awe.

The reserves of Highland timber came into use at exactly the right time for Lowland Scots and English iron smelters. They were discovered with the failure of the '15 Rising, when General Wade drove his roads into previously inaccessible areas. English laws against the smelting of iron with wood had to be obeyed, but the Scottish laws of forest protection were disregarded. Within a short time bloomeries had been established all over Scotland, new opportunities arising with the failure of the '45. At the time of maximum production at Bonawe it is probable that over a hundred bloomeries were working in Scotland.

Corpach, at the head of Loch Linnhe, where the present pulp mill is situated, was an important wharf for landing iron-ore from England, whence it was carried to Loch Lochy, and eventually to Invergarry for smelting in the forest. From Abernethy to Loch Maree the woods were being converted to charcoal. Never was one country so denuded of so much natural timber in so short a time.

But even to the exploiter all good things come to an end. The ponies laden with panniers of charcoal were having to walk farther and farther as the forest was cleared. The writing was on the wall for Highland iron-smelting when the Carron Iron Works found it cheaper to bring the trees from Glen Moriston to Falkirk than to site the furnace among the trees as in the past.

The Lorn Furnace is a monument to one kind of destruction. The work of deforestation was to go on as woodlands were set alight to make grazings for sheep introduced as the iron-men departed. And when sheep failed to live up to their promise, the estates were bought up by the new rich of the industrial revolution to become deer forests and grouse moors. The mats of alien conifers now reclothing the hillsides of Loch Awe and Loch Etive are brave attempts to redress the balance, but they are no substitute for the oaks and Caledonian pines which have been lost. Already they are feeding the pulp mill at Corpach.

Oban deserves its reputation as being one of the finest touring and sailing centres in the Western Highlands: open to the islands, served by good car ferries and backed by the lochs and glens I have described. Market for Hebridean livestock and a busy landing port for a big fleet of fishing boats, it is on a hub of Highland life with plenty to keep the visitor interested: golf, sailing, water skiing, whisky distilling, a tweed mill, a seaweed factory, pipe band, dancing and day excursions to islands as far away as Iona. You can even drive on to Seil Island by Atlantic Bridge and drive across it, ferrying over to Luing if you feel like it. From that point only the Sound of Luing separates you from Scarba and the Gulf of Corryvreckan.

I remember one evening on the top of Cnoic Mor of Luing, which I had climbed to watch the sunset. But it was the spectacle of the tide driving the waters out of the Firth of Lorn into the Sound of Jura which held my eye. The currents were moving on the water like rivers, as if the sea was on a slope. You could almost feel the pent-up force of water gathering between the maze of black islands.

There is a lobster pond on Luing, where something like 40,000 are stored inside walls built between two islands. Unfortunately I could not talk to the man who looks after this enterprise for an east coast owner who buys the lobsters when they are at their cheapest and keeps them in the pond until the price is right. That man was away on Lunga, erecting a railing round the grave of St Columba's mother, I was told. The last piece of information was given in such a matter-of-fact way that you would have thought she had died yesterday.

The pink granite cathedral in Oban is dedicated to St Columba, which is appropriate, with Iona, the most sacred isle in Christendom, lying almost due west beyond the Ross of Mull. Sailing to it is easy, by day excursion leaving Oban at 9 a.m., arriving at 1 p.m. and allowing roughly two hours ashore, or you can take a ship to Craignure with your car and drive through Mull to cross the Sound of Iona by ferry-boat. It was by the latter route I went on my last trip on a wild September day of rain.

I had been looking forward to climbing Ben More on Mull, the only 3,000-ft peak in the Hebrides outside the Cuillins of Skye, but, since the day was unworthy of it, we passed on for a consolation prize in the Gribun Rocks which I would not have missed. This is a place where the Loch na Keal road is squeezed by the mighty cliff above, on to a mere shelf above the sea. A notice warns you of rock-fall danger, but there is nothing you can do about it except note the big blocks which have landed above and below the road. One big boulder on the east side is known as the Lovers' Stone, because it occupies ruins where there used to be a cottage.

A tree grows from the stones beside it now, and the story is told that the stone fell on a newly-married couple on their wedding night. I spoke to the shepherd here, a cheery-faced man. 'It happened long before my time. But the rocks still come down when we get this kind of weather.'

A different world, when you turn the corner and climb over the hill into Gleann Seilisdeir, where the Forestry Commission trees seem to be doing well on gentler ground. But I wondered about the economics of harvesting them as we contoured the narrow road round Loch Scridain and followed it down to the Ross of Mull, the highway getting wider and smoother as we neared Iona. We were in luck to catch the midday ferry, even if there was no cover in the open boat in the pelting rain, and we were glad to get inside the only hotel open.

The magic of Iona is in its changes of weather. That grey day never let up. We went to bed in a noise of wind and rain. The morning broke calm and warm with the clarity and colour that you get only after storm. Now we could savour the two little worlds of Iona, the fringe of green fields peppered with yellow corn stacks above white sands, and the acid interior with its tawny moor grass and outcropping rock skeletons, reminiscent of Sutherland, Staffa and the Dutchman's Cap, were almost the blue of the sea that day, and west you could look over the Bay at the Back of the Ocean to the spray of breakers beyond the farming fields.

The cathedral, seen against the shining pink granite of the Ross of Mull, looked very much grander than when I saw it last. It had even acquired a new monument, a replica of St John's Cross, but it seemed to me to compare feebly with St Martin's Cross, whose embossed stone seems to hark back far into time. The restoration of the ruined cathedral and its buildings is a wonderful success story which began in 1938, when Dr George F. MacLeod, MC, DD, resigned his church in Govan and with six other ministers of the Church of Scotland came to Iona to found a community and try to discover how the teachings of Celtic Christianity could keep pace with a rapidly changing social order and become again a force in Scotland.

Dr MacLeod, very much a realist, faced the fact that three-quarters of the population of Scotland no longer went to church, and that almost the whole work of the ministry was devoted to the spiritual needs of the odd quarter.

What was wanted, he felt, was a missionary crusade—not in the Billy Graham manner, but rather in the manner of St Columba who came to Iona over 1,400 years ago to bring Christian civilization to his adopted land and founded his teaching on the relationship between work and worship. Columba did not merely talk but built, acted, advised, preached, and was such a force among men that he not only created peace between warring Pictish tribes but was given the task of selecting a king for Scotland.

That was Scotland in the time of Aidan, appointed King of Dalriada and the first monarch in Britain to be consecrated by royal coronation.

The Iona Community went to Iona as builders, to work and worship. There were the ruins of an abbey church, the only one of its kind in the world where people of any denomination could hold their full services. To rebuild these ruins would be work for the hands. To recreate the message of St Columba and apply its work and worship principles to modern life, distil it through workshops and factories, housing schemes and industrial belts, would be work for the heart.

The new-found Iona Community were seeking ministers fresh from divinity halls, boys and girls reaching manhood, workers, craftsmen and churchmen from all walks of life; and it got them, as I saw when I lived with the Community as a guest 16 years after its conception. We lived a very full life.

For example while craftsmen, ministers and guests were building with stone and wood within and without the rising Abbey block, lectures might be taking place on theology or industry or the Christian influence in trade unionism. Elsewhere a party might be engaged in dismantling an old house or a wall, bought by the Community for its weathered stones, while north and south in two camps were about 80 of the happiest and noisiest boys and girls you could meet, yet abandoning football, swimming and exploring for morning bible study round their tents and evening worship in the Abbey. Hundreds come to the camps every year, mostly from youth clubs or church groups, but anyone may apply.

The Refectory, built with New Zealand money and gifted Norwegian timber, is superbly finished with massive oak tables and forms. The wall of the Cloisters now stands whole, and on it is mounted a belfry with a historic bell weighing 2 cwt. Evidence points to it having hung at the Palace of St Stephen's Westminster, calling Oliver Cromwell to prayer. It was cast in 1540 by Peter Vanden Ghein of Malines. America gave the money for the Cloisters, and South Africa for St Michael's Chapel.

It was on a Sunday, after Communion service which is held every week in Iona, that I first got to know Dr MacLeod. He took me on a visit to the Hermit's Cell which faces Tiree and the Treshnish Isles, and may have been St Columba's private place of prayer. On the green turf were the circular ruins of a hut and near it what Dr Mac-Leod believed to be a Druid circle, complete with altar, the only sign remaining of the sun-worshippers who inhabited Iona before the coming of the saint.

Sitting on the sun-warmed stones I learnt, how the whole project of rebuilding the Abbey and founding the summer headquarters of the Community depended on finding a water supply, and how, despite the efforts of water diviners from the mainland, no water could be found. But on the very day when the water diviners were due to depart the steamer was delayed and they returned to the Abbey, passing their waiting time by digging in the old well in the hope of finding coins flung there for luck. By the time they were due to leave the island they had found not coins but the water on which the community now depends.

I was told, too, how the beautiful silver Celtic cross that distinguishes the communion table came into the possession of the Community. By chance Dr MacLeod went with a friend to the sale of effects of a deceased silversmith. His friend wanted to give a gift to the Community if something suitable could be found. In a corner, out of the way, was this cross, but it was not for sale. The widow of the craftsman was keeping it because her husband had designed it as a labour of love to be placed in the Abbey of Iona.

It was a superb afternoon as we walked the rough ground of the west coast, grey rocks, purple heather and a sea of green stretching beyond white sands to the infinite distances of Labrador 2,000 miles away. We circled round to look down on the Ridge of Kings, where, overlooking the Sound of Iona and the white cottages of Fionnphort, are buried Macbeth and Duncan, his victim, with 57 other kings of Scotland, Ireland and Norway.

To this shore, where pre-Christian Celts worshipped the rising sun and kept the Feast of Beltane, Columba brought Christianity while Rome was still pagan. From here he and his men had gone on their missions, converting the Picts by peace, when they had withstood the legions of Rome in war.

Below us were the medieval ruins of St Oran's Chapel, dating back to the eleventh century, oldest building on the island, now re-roofed and beautifully restored. South of it are the reddish stones of the nunnery occupied by Benedictine nuns who lived on in peace even after the Reformation. Of St Columba's foundation there is no sign. The most ancient buildings are modern compared to his collection of timber and wattle huts surrounded by earthworks and occupied by men who were not recluses but navigators, farmers, and craftsmen who sailed the seas to carry their civilizing crafts as well as teach the gospel.

Little is known today about the theology of the Celtic Church, but Presbyterians, Episcopalians, and Roman Catholics claim affinity with St Columba, which is the reason why all of them may hold services in the Abbey Church.

During my stay with the Iona Community I saw the moving ceremony of a number of young campers coming before the congregation to make public their belief in God. Among them was a young university student who earlier in the week had told me he was an agnostic. On a more recent visit to the island in late autumn I shared the hotel lounge with two members of the Jewish religious sect known as Essenes, who at midnight departed to hold their own service in the Abbey.

The story of Iona is not all peace and kindness. The Vikings ushered in the dark era in 795 with the first of their robbing, murdering and destroying raids, causing the island to be abandoned after 86 monks had been massacred in 806. Occupied again, it was raided twice more, in 825 and 986, with more massacres. In the eleventh century Iona was under the Norwegian diocese of Man and the Isles, when King Duncan and Macbeth were buried. In the twelfth century it came under Trondjem, but this did not save it from being plundered by Norse pirates. By that time Celtic Christianity had been replaced by Roman Catholicism and in 1263 King Hakon had been defeated at the Battle of Largs.

It was the son of the great Somerled, Reginald of Islay, who rebuilt the monastery for Black Monks and founded the nunnery of pink stone which is now such a stately ruin. The monks were expelled in 1561 at the Reformation, but the nuns were allowed to live on until 1574 when Iona passed to the Macleans of Duart. The modern Abbey incorporates the old. Its cathedral status lasted from *c.* 1500 until 1560, when dismantling began.

Church and State had troubled times thereafter between the Episcopacy and the Presbytery. Charles I voted £400 for the restoration of the Abbey in 1635, but by 1638 the Episcopacy had been abolished. Inevitably it passed into the hands of the Duke of Argyll in the seventeenth century, though in 1745 the Iona people sided with Jacobite Prince Charlie and not with Hanoverian Argyll. The Duke gave Iona Abbey in trust to the Church of Scotland in 1899 on the understanding that all denominations could use it. The Abbey itself was restored in the first decade of this century.

The south-west coast of Iona is, in my view, the most neglected and most beautiful section of an enchanting island, from the 'Bay at the Back of the Ocean' one looks through the rocky gap of Temple Glen to a turfy oasis on the Atlantic edge.

Here fringing the sea is the land without which St Columba could not have founded his mission church, and here in half a mile are the colours of the island at their most varied, from machair brilliant with flowers and silver sands, to gleaming pink rocks above waves which can be green, blue, puple, hyacinth, according to the light falling upon them from the vast arch of sky above.

To watch skerries being engulfed in every seventh wave and hear the roar of their tempestuous charge is exciting, but not until you investigate what looks like a tremendous waterspout at the edge of the bay can you appreciate the full force of the sea.

This is Iona's famous spouting cave, a rock chimney like a pipe, into which the sea is sucked to be spat out in a spraying jet high into the sky. The force of the projection depends on the size of the wave, but it can go up over a hundred feet, with an explosive sound as the air pressure acts like a loud gasping breath.

To approach the cave when it is spouting you should watch which way the wind is blowing, else you will be soaked in its spray some time before you are alongside. Trying to take a photograph there one day I found myself looking up at an otter dancing over the rocks above me. It was in a hurry and brought its bounding motion to a halt only on the very brink of the rock chimney forming the cave. Then it dived into the welter of boiling surf below. The cave spouted, and I half-expected to see an otter projected from its top—but, no. There it was, a dark form in the foam, a blunt face and waving sharp point of tail as it let itself be thrown about, master of its environment and enjoying it.

The fine autumn weather was still holding when we left Iona to cross the narrow sound to Fionnphort in Mull, where we had left the car. A perfect day for Ben More, the fields of Balmeanach smooth as carpets under black headlands. It was easy to see how Mull is made up of great terraces of volcanic rock which break down into good soil. Amid a landscape spattered with cattle, and fronted by Ulva and Staffa, the white houses seemed wonderfully attractive places to stay. The farming is good. It is the problems of freight and transport which makes survival difficult. But the emptiness of Mull is an artificial condition resulting from the expulsion of its people to make way for sheep. In the 224,788 acres of Mull the population is only five to the square mile, yet its green fertility is the envy of the Highlands.

The rot began when this cattle country suffered a colonial-style change with the large-scale introduction of sheep, and the unwanted tenantry were forced to emigrate. Maybe Mull was overpopulated at 10,612 persons in 1821. It was grossly underpopulated in 1961 at 2,343, by which time it was carved into small estates owned by wealthy Englishmen as retreats from the world. It is still a placid backwater when it could be something more vital and vigorous.

Yet Mull has been discovered, and in the summer bursts with tourists, landed at Craignure by car ferry. With 135 miles of narrow but reasonably surfaced roads and perhaps the finest anchorage in the Hebrides for touring yachtsmen, it has all the scenic variety of an island deeply cut by lochs and protruding headlands. I wanted to see it from the top of Ben More, the highest piece of tertiary basalt in Britain, so went round to Loch na Keal and at Dishig saw a sign pointing to the path.

The route follows up the burn, which spills in waterfalls over every rock terrace. The sheep track is easy to walk on until you come to an incipient ravine, where you take to the shoulder of the hill. Drifting puffs of cloud were breaking round the stony summit when we got there, acting as screens on which our shadows walked, circled with rainbow, flickering bright or dimming according to the density of the mist screen. This strange effect is known as a 'glory' and occurs when the sun uses the climber's body like a slide in a projector and the mist acts as a screen. It is the water droplets acting as prisms which create the colour rings of rainbow. It is by no means as rare as is often made out. We could enjoy the glories all the more for the fine visibility on each side of the puff balls of mist, with peaks of the Cuillins of Skye standing out to the north and the houses of Oban visible to the east. You could appreciate how wild the centre of Mull is, from the great wilderness of Ardmeanach, spanned only by adventurous paths, to the clustering peaks round Loch Ba. How different this centre part of Mull is from the granite of the Ross to the south and the woodlands of Salen and Tobermory to the north.

Tobermory has a population of over 600, ranged round one of the safest and most attractive harbours in all the West. Facing east towards Morvern and Ardnamurchan, nature has even provided an island in the mouth of the bay for added shelter. Summer brings the yachtsmen, arriving from the Sound of Mull or from the Western Isles, for this is a cruising centre *par excellence*.

You can play golf here and, as you walk across the links, speculate on the whereabouts of the Spanish Armada treasure said to lie in the bottom of the bay only eighty yards off shore. The tale is that there is £300,000 in gold pieces down there, sunk when Maclean of Duart acted too hastily by blowing up the ship, when the skipper refused to pay him blackmail money. That was 400 years ago. Salvage attempts have been made over the years, and small finds have been made under 11 fathoms of water. The treasure remains an exciting mystery.

But the real treasure of Mull in these distant days was the land. Mull was a main source of cattle and its drove roads were used by other beasts landed from Coll and Tiree on the big trek to Perth and Falkirk by Loch Awe, Inveraray or alternative routes described in the last chapter. Cattle were also thieved from other islands by the Macleans of Duart, as in 1579 when 500 beasts and 2,000 sheep and goats were purported to be lifted from Gigha. He must have had a considerable fleet to get them home.

The route to market for the cattle was by Grass Point to Kerrera, from which islands the beasts swam across the narrow strait to the mainland, or by Salen to Mishnish, where they were ferried across the Sound of Mull to the Morven shore. Another bit of eighteenth-century traffic was charcoal for the Lorn furnace, as birch, ash and oak woods went up in flames on Mull.

Clansmen of these days had to be sailors, as able at handling boats as working the land. I discovered how thoroughly the sea-going tradition had died when I tried all over Mull to find someone to take me out to the Treshnish Isles in October. I wanted to study Atlantic seals and stay for a few days on these volcanic isles lying west of Ulva. I had to give up the idea. I did find an old man in Calgary who said he was prepared to go, but when morning came he had changed his mind.

CHAPTER FIVE

Fort William, Ben Nevis and Ardnamurchan

Lochaber—Fort William—Ben Nevis—Ardgour and Ardnamurchan—Loch Shiel and Morvern

Whichever way you explore the West Highlands, Fort William is a key point in its topography, a parting of important ways: open to the Atlantic at Loch Linnhe; connected to the North Sea at Inverness by canal and low-level road through the Great Glen; linked to the fishing port of Mallaig by rail and road for Skye and the Small Isles; while eastward Loch Laggan leads to the Spey Valley by Newtonmore and Aviemore. Small wonder the town of Fort William began its life as a military fort and that today it is a bustling town expanding round to Loch Eil.

Fort William was important in the subjugation of the Highlands because it could be supplied by sea, a vital consideration before General Wade began his road-building programme in 1725. From Oban the motorist has a choice of two exciting approaches. One is by car ferry to Lochaline on the Sound of Mull for a trip through remote Morvern and Ardgour, crossing Loch Linnhe by Corran Ferry. The alternative is northward by Benderloch and Strath Appin to Ballachulish for a short crossing of Loch Leven, or to detour round the length of this narrow fjord and add twenty miles. A varied choice of accommodation is available on the final lap between Onich and Fort William.

My first arrival in the town was less orthodox. Weighed down by heavy rucksacks, two of us had walked from Taynuilt railway station on the Oban line up the length of Loch Etive. Then after a night in camp we had crossed a pass into Glen Coe to hit the zigzags of the Devil's Staircase climbing north over the hills to Kinlochleven. It was by this route Hamilton's support troops had marched on the morning of the Massacre to cut off the escape routes of the MacDonalds. But the snow which had fallen in the night delayed them until eleven o'clock, by which time the deed was done and the lucky ones had escaped. Today the route links up with the great pipes carrying water from the Blackwater Reservoir to the aluminium works at Kinlochleven. The town, crouched beneath the steep hills hemming the loch, is a sunless and wet place.

Fort William is hardly any drier, but it is infinitely cheerier, though the density of traffic jamming its long narrow street has reached thrombosis point. Ben Nevis was our target on that first visit, but what possessed us to camp half way up it, and carry our rucksacks right over the top, still baffles me. It was purgatorial, and frightening in the mist, when we tried to come down the rocky far side in order to climb Aonach Beag. After that we slogged through the hills to Rannoch Moor via Loch Treig.

In many subsequent visits, one day stands out from all the rest.

It is an April morning. Len and I are stirring out of our sleeping bags before even the first birds have started to sing. The sky has a clear hardness after a night of frost; and though we hate early rising as much as the next man we do it cheerfully because we are camping in Glen Nevis and have a fair way to go to reach the soaring ridges of the north-east face which give the longest rock and ice climbs in mainland Britain.

We are off at 6.50 a.m., a good breakfast of coffee, bacon and eggs inside us. We move fast in the keen air, up the zigzags of the path, then leave it at the Lochan Meall an't Suidhe to contour round the mountain into the wintry north side. Revelation when we round Carn Dearg and look up at the cracked, splintered, ribbed and castellated face soaring 2,000 ft over our heads, the cornices pendulus like overgenerous ice-cream cones. Underfoot the snow is crisp after frost and the pale green sky is clear of cloud.

We might be in the Alps, coming up to some magnificently placed cabin, we reflect, as we approach the Scottish Mountaineering Club hut. Perched below the jutting edges of Scotland's three greatest ridges, it is in a position to command the whole two-mile expanse of Gothic architecture which is this cathedral face. Friends of ours are inside the hut, having just risen to make their breakfast, but we do not

15 *This puffer uses an age-old route from Loch Etive by the Falls of Lora to the sea. The cargo is granite chippings for road building in Mull*

16 *Highland shepherd above Glen Creran*

stay to talk to them, because they tell us they are bound for the
Observatory Ridge, and we want a flying start on them. The time is
9 a.m., and we have to cut steps with our axes to reach the foot of the
ridge.

Observatory Ridge is perhaps the stateliest ridge of Nevis. Beginning as an incipient buttress, it rises steep and continues for 2,000
ft, tapering as it rises to true edge, soaring above the spectacular rock
scenery of the face.

We have made no plan of attack. We know each other too well for
that, and as we rope, by tacit consent we shorten our line; each man
takes a few coils in one hand and we move off together. This is the
Alpine method of climbing, unlike the British method where only
one man moves at a time; and it is only justifiable when both men are
equally competent on the kind of terrain they are climbing. It is
exhilarating because it cuts out waiting, and it calls for constant
vigilance in handling the rope, to take up slack, or avoid jerking your
companion. We are making height fast, because the steps cut by an
Easter party of a few days before have frozen into cups and we can
use them as hand or foot-holds without having to recut them with our
axes.

Not until the ridge narrows for its final rise to the summit do our
axes come into full play. The previous party appears to have traversed
off the ridge into Zero Gully in preference to keeping on its edge,
which now rises as a fragile leaf of snow, and we have good sport
cutting a way up it, scraping the steep rocks clear of ice until all that
lies before us is the corniced edge of the summit. Eating a sandwich
and revelling in a view that embraces silvery lochs and the deep
trenches of Scotland's finest glens, we give up trying to sort out the
welter of snow-dappled peaks stretching from Ben Lomond to the
Cuillins of Skye.

The time is only 11.30 a.m. The day is young yet, and we feel like
some more climbing so up along the cornice we go, examining the
frightening overhangs poised to avalanche when the thaw comes.

The plan now, we decide, is to descend the Tower Ridge, and
we are glad of well-cut steps down the cornice to the Tower Gap.
When iced, this gap can be an awkward problem, since it is a vertical
cleft which there is no avoiding. But today it is dry and straightforward,
and once across it we try to descend the north face of the Great

17   *Mist swirls over Ben More, 3,169 ft, the highest peak in Mull*
18   *St Columba's Bay, Iona, landing place of the most famous of the
     Celtic saints*

Tower—which is our mistake, because the true route is down the east side. The snow here—what there is of it—has been catching the sun, and is soft and unreliable, but we are soon on to clean rocks again, and moving down this glorious rock staircase.

We chat to some members of the Inverness Mountaineering Club we meet on their way up the ridge, and as we climb down the last vertical chimney, Len has an idea. 'Why not make a hat trick and finish off the day by climbing the North-East Buttress? We could do it and be back in camp by 7 p.m.,' he says. 'And we'll have stolen two weekends out of one.'

It is an attractive idea, not because it is a hat trick, but because Slingsby's Chimney is mostly snow-filled, and it promises a sporting route if we can use it to gain the crest of the First Platform. We race across to it, and are soon hacking a way up it. There is a little ice pitch and an overhanging block to negotiate, then we are on difficulties where only one man dare move at a time. The lead happens to be mine, and I watch every step, testing every rock hold because the situation is exposed and I rate the rock here as being dangerously brittle.

The hold-up costs us half an hour more than we bargained for, but once on the crest we can move fast again on its delightful upper section, and are soon faced with the obstacle known as the 'Mantrap'. Len leads this tilting groove with as much spring in his muscles as if he were just starting the day. But I know and feel in my muscles that I have done nearly 6,000 ft of rock climbing, and admit relief when the angle eases and we are again on top—to the surprise of the Inverness Mountaineering Club members who reckon that these Glasgow climbers certainly like value for their money.

We reflected that away back in 1892, when Professor Norman Collie stepped on to the top of Ben Nevis, having made the first complete ascent of Tower Ridge, his party were able to walk a few steps and refresh themselves inside Britain's only mountain-top observatory. Collie the scientist would not be too full of his climb to miss the chance of talk about natural phenomena to the pioneer weathermen who for a dozen years had been taking hour-by-hour readings on the summit of the mountain, recording the amazing fluctuations of wind and temperature which showed this to be amongst the most troubled spots on the face of the earth.

Perhaps they discussed Clement Wragge, who climbed Ben Nevis every day for two summers before the observatory was built, Wragge, the 4 a.m. riser, who set off from sea level every day taking instrument readings at various stages to arrive on top about 9 a.m. Thus he was able to build up over a long period the graphic differences which are created by altitude and exposure to Atlantic weather disturbances. Wragge soon discovered that tolerable conditions at sea level could become impossible in wind and rain on the summit plateau.

History records him as the first long-range weather forecaster in the world, and it was through his zeal that the money to build the Ben Nevis Observatory was found. I am glad to say the £4,000 required was raised in Scotland, and in five months of intensive work his dream became a reality. A round-the-clock weather station had been established to be enlarged to four rooms with conning tower to project through the snows which completely covered the first building.

The observatory became a great draw. Thousands of visitors walked up the pony track to see it. University students and others worked in it for no more than their board and lodgings. One of them was Charles Wilson, a Scottish physicist who won a Nobel prize. Lord Kelvin and other men of note praised the original work being done on the top of Ben Nevis, but the Government would not pay the £1,000 a year necessary to keep the station manned; they gave it only £350 a year. So, on the very eve of the aeroplane age, when weather science was to have new significance, the instruments were dismantled and the shutters put up. The diamond jubilee of this dismal decision occurred in 1964. In the circumstances it is not surprising that Mr Wragge went to Australia, to become a famous meteorologist there, and to found another observatory, this time on the top of Mount Kosciusko in the Blue Mountains.

So we raised our woollen hats to the ruins on the plateau, regarding it as Wragge's monument. And we marvelled at his zeal as we jolted down the stony pony track which seems to go on forever. Innocent as it looks, people have been killed on these simple slopes in winter though the majority of deaths have occurred on the north side of the mountain. Nevis has accounted for more climbers than the North Face of the Eiger: no fewer than 31 died in a ten-year period. None were casual tourists. All had the pretence of being climbers, in that they were semi-experienced or were upon the mountain under some sort of experienced leadership. It must be bluntly stated that most of them died because they underrated the savagery of Ben Nevis weather and the complicated topography of the mountain.

The big pipes that sprout out of Ben Nevis empty from 15 miles of tunnel bored to Loch Treig. This generates the electricity for the aluminium factory and when work began in 1924 it seemed a mighty undertaking. The tunnel set a world record for length and the hydro-electric scheme was the biggest that had been attempted in Britain. It marked the beginning of Fort William as a growth point. The latest addition is the giant pulp mill at Corpach just round the bay.

Invited to give a lecture to the Scottish Pulp Mountaineering Club I got a chance to meet a number of the workers and be taken on a tour of the mill. The climbers, mostly from Glasgow and other towns, were happy to be in the Highlands and did not mind the four-shift system, with a wage of around £2,000 a year. 'You don't think about weekends any more,' said Donald Watt, President of the Club. 'My two days off are Thursday and Friday this week, and I'm off with three work-mates tomorrow. That's the advantage of having our own club. We can always get climbing companions.'

Arriving at the mill I had seen the two great mountains of material which I took to be sawdust, one of them being given a pointed shape by a spray-gun of matter shot from the end of a pipe high above it. The pile was composed of minced trees in the form of chips, and the process of conversion from tree to chips was one of the most frightening things I have ever seen.

First the bark is removed from the logs, then they are carried along a conveyor belt into a great shed like a stone-crushing plant to slide down a chute. The frightening bit is the whirling blade which meets the log and in one second tears it apart, shredding it to chips and shooting them through pressure pipes to be sprayed on the pile outside. The two mountains of chippings side by side were of different materials, one was of hardwood chips, darker in colour than the neighbouring softwood. The bark which had been stripped off was on its way by another pipe to fuel the powerhouse, helping to produce enough electricity to supply a town the size of Perth.

The powerhouse is a tall tower belching white smoke with an acrid smell. It burns not only bark and oil, but also residual chemicals too dangerous to be dumped in the sea. From now on I was to see the integrated process of converting wood chips to pulp and fine paper which is unique in Britain, for there is no other plant capable of the linked chain from raw materials to perfectly finished product.

I began to appreciate why Corpach cost £15 million and had a host of teething troubles in the first three years between 1966 and 1969, with banks of instruments, including closed-circuit television, for controlling the process of transforming wood chips to pulp and then to fast-moving rolls of paper.

The chips go into five great digesters, which could be likened to pressure cookers, to be reduced not by steam but by chemicals to crude pulp in eleven hours. Now follow mechanical screening, washing, and five stages of bleaching and more washing until the pulp is in white rolls like cotton wool. A most important factor in the total economics of the mill is that the expensive chemicals can be used again, a vital saving in pollution as well as money.

John Currie, microscopist, gave further insight. 'Think of a tree as being countless millions of fibres held together by a sort of plastic. The plastic is the lignin, and forms 25 per cent of the tree; the rest is cellulose fibres. To produce good quality paper the lignin has to be removed, hence the cooking process. Paper is possible because cellulose fibres naturally bond together when dry.

'A mixture of hardwood and softwood fibres produces the best paper. My job is to study the fibre content of papers to supply information which will enable the mill to produce the kind of paper required by the customers. You learn how to read the fibres. It's quite fun to be able to recognize a spruce, a pine or a larch by a tiny bit under the microscope.' John is a climber and naturalist. He was a good man to ask about the pollution factor. Did it worry him?

He was categorical that there was no need to worry; this on the evidence from the Scottish Marine Biological Station who surveyed Loch Linnhe and Loch Eil before the mill was set up, and have been surveying it ever since. In fact, the marine life has noticeably increased, so it may be that the mill is having a fertilizing effect. The burning of the toxic waste, the re-use of the chemicals and the careful screening and discharge of effluent at suitable tides have reduced the pollution hazard to a minimum, though there must, inevitably, be some air pollution from the smoke.

The work-force is 950 and in 1974 it is planned to put in another gigantic paper-making machine which means that the mill could turn out 25 miles of paper per hour. Amazingly, these automated machines need only three men to attend the instruments.

The West Highland Railway has been crucial to the success story of the pulp mill, with Crianlarich as the key centre for special timber trains to Corpach. Because of the inadequate roads, the mill would not have been sited in its present location without the railway. Timber ships from North America can sail up Loch Linnhe, while from the North Sea smaller ships can pass through the Caledonian Canal. Unfortunately the quality of housing developments do not match their setting, as I saw when I visited some of the workers.

Yet all admitted that they were happier here and better housed than they had ever been in Glasgow. I remember the gleam of light in the eyes of one young climber when he said to me:

'Imagine, only $2\frac{1}{4}$ hours from Corpach to Sligachan in Skye; Ardgour in an hour; the Cairngorms in $1\frac{1}{2}$ hours; Torridon in $2\frac{1}{2}$ hours, and Glen Nevis any time after work on day shift!' Given the jobs, more people would leave the Central Belt for the West Highlands. Of that I am sure.

Fort William, as such, began its life in 1654, 38 years before the Massacre of Glen Coe, when General Monck, acting for Cromwell, built a fort and called it Inverlochy. It was the beginning of the pacification of the Highlands, work which was to be furthered in the reign of King William of Orange when MacKay repaired the fort and renamed it Maryburgh, after the first lady in the land. The wife has been forgotten but William is remembered though even the fort has vanished.

It was dismantled to build the railway. The real Inverlochy which prompted General Monck to use this name for his fort stands two miles north of the town near the aluminium factory and dates much further back, to the Comyn family who in the thirteenth century were given the lordship of Badenoch and Lochaber, controlling it from the castles at Lochindorb, Inverlochy and Blair Atholl. In addition to these castles there was also a mote at Ruthven.

The thirteenth-century castle on the River Lochy, situated close to the aluminium factory, should be visited, not merely because it is a well preserved early castle with quadrangular wall and round angle towers with bow slits, but because this is the site of one of the most enterprising victories in Highland history, achieved after a mid-winter journey across some of the most difficult country in the north.

The victor was the Great Montrose leading a charge of 1,800 Highlanders and Irish against Argyll's Covenanting army. The date was 31 January when Montrose, camped at the foot of Loch Ness, heard the news that the Campbells were at Inverlochy with an army nearly twice the size of his own. And cutting him off from the north was an even bigger army at Inverness.

He chose to engage at Inverlochy but not by marching back the way he had come. Due eastward of him was a glen leading to the bare heights of the Corrieyairack, deep in mid-winter snow at over 2,500 ft. Beyond it in a hollow lies tiny Loch Spey, the source of the great river, and just west of the loch Glen Roy opens westward beyond a low pass.

That was the route he marched his men over, tramping night and day. Down on the low ground of Glen Spean he then led his men along the north flanks of the Ben Nevis range to achieve complete suprise on the morning of 2 February. Argyll, the MacChailein Mor, fled, nor could his army, with their slow-firing muskets, withstand the sword charge of Montrose's royalist force. Argyll's army was smashed, but MacChailein Mor was to have the last laugh for he lived to see Montrose hanged five years later.

The brilliant victories of Montrose came just three months too late to win Scotland for King Charles I. But the Covenanters lost too, because of their attempts to impose their religion on the country. With a cry of 'Jesus and no quarter' they could massacre prisoners, women and children. It happened at Philipshaugh when Montrose's army was cut to pieces. And it persisted until Cromwell's military government enforced religious toleration. It was then that General Monck built his fort, which was to become known as Fort William, on the site at Inverlochy.

The railway that destroyed the old military fort was opened in 1894, reaching the town from the north-east after curving round the Ben Nevis range. Emerging into Glen Spean at Tulloch it passes the entrance to Glen Roy and follows the rough line taken by Montrose when he swooped on Argyll at Inverlochy. The West Highland Railway, for much of its way, tracks across a route unspanned by any road.

The wildest part of the line is from Bridge of Orchy, where a steel horse-shoe of viaduct is carried on tall stilts beneath Ben Dorain. Perched on its slender crest, the diesel train appears to an onlooker as a mere toy, and this feeling is shared by the passengers who, by merely looking out of the window, can see the front and rear of the train at the same time, so tight is the curve.

Rannoch Moor lies just ahead, a wilderness unspanned by any highway, except at its western extremity, where the Glen Coe road climbs over the Black Mount. The elevated mattress of peat, rocks and trailing lochs was a formidable problem to the builders. The railway picks its way across the spongier bits on viaducts; one of them with nine clear spans is 684 ft long. At other points the foundation has been built upon tree roots of former forest covered with brushwood and thousands of tons of rocks and ashes.

The rail journey across the Moor is saved from monotony by its vistas of peaks, lochs and rivers. Golden eagles, herds of red deer, coveys of grouse, or a fast-flying merlin may be seen if you watch out. Snow barriers restrict the views in places, and for 205 yards the train passes through a cutting roofed with corrugated iron to prevent blockage in blizzards. This is Britain's only snowshed, and it lies just north of Rannoch Station.

North of this is Corrour Passing-Place, with nothing each side of it except the wild mountains of Ben Alder to the east and the Mamore Forest peaks to the west. Away to the left is Ben Nevis. Reflect as you pass unsightly Loch Treig that these are the waters carried by pipes and tunnel through Ben Nevis to power the aluminium factory in Fort William. The last lap is through territory of Brae-Lochaber, well named, since you are passing beneath the highest ground in Scotland. There is much to look out for between Tulloch, where the train turns west, and Fort William station on the seaside.

Note immediately above Tulloch on the north side a grassy road running along the hillside like a contour line. It is one of the shore lines left by a great lake which filled the valley in ice-age times when a glacier debouched from the Nevis range to block Glen Spean. The last big advance of ice is given as between 15,000 and 20,000 years ago.

To see three distinct shore lines you have to go up Glen Roy where the 'road' levels are at 1,149, 1,068 and 857 ft. The highest represents the peak glaciation, and as the ice melted the level fell until finally the water leaked away. You get a fine impression of them from a big car park above the crofts of Glen Roy.

The 'roads', which look so even from a distance, prove to be not so flat when you climb up to them, but have a rough inclination due to shelving. You can drive near to the head of Glen Roy, and if you have a mind, walk across to the Spey drainage to look Corrieyairack-wards where Montrose crossed on his epic march. It may be his men used the 'roads' for easy travelling.

The glaciological origin of these roads was not guessed at until the middle of last century. British scientists thought they had been caused by changing sea level or floods of a biblical character. Then along came Louis Agassiz of Switzerland who saw everywhere around him the litter left by glaciers in the course of their melting. It marked the beginning of a new understanding and interpretation of Highland landscape whose deep lochs are rock basins dug by glacial ice.

Ben Nevis is a classic example of a Scottish volcanic peak modified by the action of ice-cap and glacier. And Spean Bridge is the perfect place to view its north-eastern corrie. Look up and take notice of the thrust of these cliffs forming nearly half the height of the mountain, fretted into cirques, buttresses, ridges, gullies and pinnacles—two miles of them.

The rocks are ideally suited for climbing because they were formed from masses of lava which never came to the surface as ash. The molten lava stayed inside until erosion by ice and water dug away the soft outer cover and began shaping the hard core into the intricate form which delights mountaineers today. On the other side of the mountain lies Glen Nevis and its gorge, the greatest mountain glory of Fort William. Indeed if we were to have a scale of value in terms of stars for amenity, then the gorge where the glen narrows would rank top.

All Glen Nevis is interesting, flanked by the sweep of Ben Nevis to the north, and to the south the shapely peaks of the Mamores, given distinction by their caps of quartzite greys. Thronged with campers it is touristy, it must be admitted. Campers make free of it. There is exciting roadside rock climbing at Polldubh, but as the winding road comes to an end at a big car park the true believer will know that he has just reached the gate of the promised land.

What lies behind seems scenically soft by comparison with what confronts you now, where the walls of the opposing mountains almost meet, hung with birches and Caledonian pines and framing a great waterfall spouting from a peak. The only way through is by footpath, a rock staircase in places with the Nevis thundering through great boulders below, making a sound-box of the place.

To reach such a spot in eight miles of tarred road seems something of a miracle. This is what a lady who serves teas in the glen wrote in a letter to the press, purporting to speak for the inarticulate thousands who find joy in that walk.

I guarantee that people who take that stoney track to Steall come back with a sense not only of adventure and achievement but with a compelling experience which remains with them all their days. It is not what they have seen or heard but something they have felt; it is a 'something' which they did not expect and which gives peace to the soul. This 'something' can only be found where nature can weave her undisturbed spell.

She wrote this because the North of Scotland Hydro-Electric Board were proposing to build a 240-ft high dam across Glen Nevis gorge to make a reservoir which would have submerged most of the glory. She was replying to the Board who had stated that their proposed scheme would leave natural beauty undiminished and improve access to the Glen by the building of a road up the opposite wall of the gorge. I was passionately involved in the opposition myself on the grounds that the reward in terms of electricity did not justify the rape of our finest gorge.

The National Trust for Scotland threw their weight behind the objectors and published this statement:

As it stands, the gorge is an incomparable example of the old, wild Highland landscape, contained within an area of about one square mile, which ramblers and mountaineers already know and the travellers by car can reach in 30 minutes from Fort William. The

Board's scheme involves the construction of a dam 240 ft. high. This intrusion alone will alter the scene beyond redemption and subsidiary works will inevitably cause further damage.

You should not therefore take Glen Nevis for granted when you go there. Walk through the gorge to the big waterfall. The big surprise in emerging on a great meadow, is an inner sanctuary of meandering river, walled by the big waterfall spraying from a hanging valley through rock bluffs. The little cottage of Steall under the waterfall is a climbers' hut, superbly situated for exploring the ridges on each side which link peak to peak. One man has traversed all these peaks of Brae-Lochaber in a night and June day of 1964. He was Philip Tranter who in doing the eighteen peaks climbed 20,000 ft and covered 36 miles thus girdling the mountain-ring of Glen Nevis in one continuous expedition, reaching his first peak Mullach nan Coirean at 5 p.m., and his last, Ben Nevis, at 1 p.m. 20 hours later.

Tranter was killed in a car crash all too soon after his great trip but this is what he wrote of the final stone-pile of Nevis.

Those 1,000 feet seemed never ending. The hillside faces due south, and the rocks were hot to touch, the whole place shimmering in the heat of the noonday sun—but I was utterly determined not to stop.

At one o'clock I stood by the cairn on Ben Nevis—and for an hour I owned that place. There were others about, tourists up from Fort William for the day, and climbers with ropes at the edge of the cliffs. I chatted with them, sympathising with their sorrows, their complaints about the heat and the long grind up by the track. Even had I tried I could not have convinced them that my own route was twenty times as long as theirs and included almost every mountain in the view.

I fairly ran down Ben Nevis, bounding down the boulder fields, slithering down the stony track, then straight on down through grass and bracken slopes to the River Nevis 4,000 feet below. Scorning the bridge I waded the river, and the cold of it was sheer delight on burning feet.

But you can enjoy a walk through the wildest bit of Brae-Lochaber without going for the tops. You could, for example, get dropped at the Glen Nevis car park, go through the gorge and keep following the rough path east to Loch Treig to catch the evening train at Corrour in a distance of approximately seventeen miles. Add another seven if you walk all the way from Fort William. There is a Youth Hostel at Corrour, and if you wanted to go back by another route through the hills you could spend a night there, returning to Loch Treighead next day to strike north-westwards by the Lairg Leacach path to Spean Bridge.

Fort William railway station is on the sea front, with a pier on one side and a platform on the other, and just across the water lies delightful Ardgour served by regular passenger ferry from the pier. Motorists cannot get there so easily. They have to decide whether to drive all the way round by Loch Eil or save themselves 25 miles by heading south down Loch Linnhe and making the car-ferry crossing at Corran.

Over there above Glen Tarbert lies one of Scotland's finest mountains, Garbh Bheinn, dominating the widish neck of land between Loch Linnhe and Loch Sunart, a different world of narrow roads and almost Hebridean peace, full of charm in birch woods, oaks and clumps of old pines. The summit of Garbh Bheinn is a good place for appreciating its roadless interior, and for seeing how Loch Sunart divides Morvern and Ardnamurchan.

The route to Garbh Bheinn is by the stream of Coire an Iubhair. There is a track of sorts but the true peak is hidden for a couple of miles until you swing round a shoulder and suddenly it swings into view as a bristling skyline of black rock like a piece of the Cuillins of Skye. Its most obvious feature is a swoop of rock which plunges from the summit for 1,200 ft into the Garbh Coire Mor.

What a discovery this must have been to the pioneers, J. H. Bell and W. Brown, when they climbed it in 1897. They described the ridge as being steep and sensational, with holds almost everywhere excellent. Today the climb is graded 'difficult' but anyone looking for the easiest way to the summit need only keep up the corrie to the col and reach the top without using any hands at all.

The view is the same whichever way you go, out to Rhum, Eigg Jura, Mull, Loch Sunart, even to the Arran Hills. I remember them as they were after my last ascent of the Great Ridge, all cut out of silver and black by the low position of the westering sun.

North and south there was colour: Ben Nevis, pale blue, shaped like a barrel with veins of snow as hoops; the Mamores quartz grey—

and in between these hard shades every subtle nuance from the pointed tops of Perthshire to the big ridges of Glen Shiel and Glen Affric. Long shadows modelled the shining rocks around us, heightening the tints of brown heather and green grass. From here we could see how all the glens west of Loch Linnhe lead to Loch Shiel, each spanned by a footpath, Glens Gour, Scaddle and Cona, passages through seldom-visited hills.

The Ardnamurchan peninsula, the most westerly tip of the Scottish mainland lies beyond the neck of Glen Tarbert, through the gentle strath of Carnoch then by the oaks and hazels of Loch Sunart. The car driver will be a bit too preoccupied with the windings of the single-track road fully to appreciate it, so the best plan is to stop and get out often, slipping your car off the highway where you can.

Loch Sunart means Svend's fjord, Norse of course, and it is a real gem of a sea loch, good for birds. On a spring trip I saw a great northern diver and a pair of Slavonian grebes, both species in ornate breeding plumage, and I strolled amongst the natural oaks to enjoy the clusters of violets, wood anemones and primroses which scented the air. Then on to Ardslignish where the road climbs away inland to avoid a headland called 'Maclean's Nose', sweeping 600 ft upward past a fertile bay of ruined shielings and grassy fields on the edge of white sands. The ruins tell their own story of a dwindling population which at under 1,000 for the whole peninsula is two-thirds of the 1911 figure.

We could not resist the sharp little peak of Ben Hiant only 1,200 ft above the car, once a volcano. Maclean's Nose remains the cast of its ancient crater. The climb was worth it for the view over Oronsay and Carna islands of Morvern, which form the east short shore of the Sound of Mull. West was the Island of Coll, looking very close, with northward the familiar shapes of Eigg and Rhum. The tip of the peninsula, only eight miles off now, hid its charms in an aura of superficial bleakness, dispelled when you find herds of black cattle on fine grazing and a considerable crofting township at Kilchoan curving round a bay of fields.

The bit which fascinates me however is the last six miles to the lighthouse among rocky hillocks scalped and rounded by ice-action, a peaty wild country like a fragment of Sutherland, then suddenly you are in a little strath of farmland around Loch Grigadale and a short distance off stands the pencil of the lighthouse above bays of the finest shell sand. Ardnamurchan, the 'Point of the Ocean' is well named and lies 20 miles west of the meridian of Land's End.

Here you can watch the shearwaters skimming the waves and find shelter among the rocks while watching the crash of Atlantic breakers round the lighthouse crag. Naturally the place has been discovered by caravanners, and in Sanna most of the former crofts are holiday homes. There is superb walking and rock scrambling around here, and the whole way along the north side of the Ardnamurchan peninsula to Loch Ailort by Kilmory and Kentra on tracks is splendid.

With a car, however, you have to go back along the length of Loch Sunart to Salen and take the Moidart road to Ardtoe. This whole corner is delectable for its immediate charm of white sands and views across the sea to nearby Rhum and Eigg. Ardtoe is apt to be a bit congested now because of the road and the attraction of a fish farm where plaice are raised from eggs for transfer into a three-acre salt-water farm in the sheltered corner of a creek. The fish take two years to grow to half-pound size when they are harvested. Their flavour is excellent.

Until the mid-sixties there was no coast road north of Kinlochmoidart. Motorists got this far and had to return by the way they came. Then one of the most delightful footpaths in Scotland was bulldozed to make possible a through-route along Loch Ailortside, thus linking Protestant Ardnamurchan with Roman Catholic Moidart. If you motor its scenically exciting length don't forget to make a diversion to Castle Tioram.

This MacDonald stronghold is a ruin of great character, accessible at low tide from Dorlin across easy ground. It is equally impressive if you climb the bald hill immediately overlooking it for a panoramic view of the brooding hulk of stone, screened from the west by clasping arms of tree-clad headland. It was from this hill, where I took my photograph, that Allan More of Clanranald saw his castle for the last time, in flames. He was going off to Sheriffmuir to fight for the Jacobite cause of 1715 and he caused his castle to be burned less it fall to the enemy.

The fourteenth-century castle has stood the test of time and siege, but in its long history was taken only once by an enemy, Argyll, who pierced the sea wall with cannon shot and occupied the keep when he thought Clanranald had fled. Clanranald had merely gone to collect reinforcements and returned to slaughter the Campbells doing their usual government work. Acharacle makes a fine centre for exploring the inlets of this fretted coast and motor-boat trips sometimes operate from Dorlin.

The easy way to Acharacle used to be by boat from Glenfinnan at the head of Loch Shiel, but this daily service connecting with the train no longer operates. However, a boat can be hired to take you to the seaward end of Loch Shiel for a visit to Eilean Fhianin, called after the Irish St Finnan who founded a church here. This is the burial place of the Clanranalds.

A more adventurous way into the wilds of Loch Shiel is to drive east to Strontian and cross the hills on a high, climbing and narrow track descending to Polloch village beneath the peak of Ben Resipol. All this is forestry country, and a private track now runs all the way up Loch Shiel from Polloch. On your return journey you might be interested in the mine workings where the element strontium was discovered in the lead and named after the village, Strontian.

The road to Lochaline strikes off southward round the head of Loch Sunart and across a pass through hills peppered with red deer in spring, when they have cast their antlers. The village on the Sound of Mull owes its prosperity to its sand mine, established during the Second World War and still going strong, providing silica sand for optical-glass making. Two castles hereabouts are worth looking at, the fifteenth-century Kinlochaline and fourteenth-century Ardtornish. The car-ferry service to Mull and Oban should be borne in mind. Now we look at the country between Glenfinnan and the Great Glen around which the great escape story of Prince Charlie revolved.

CHAPTER SIX

Glen Finnan, Arisaig and the Braes of Morar: Prince Charlie's Escape Country

Knoydart and the '45—the Prince as a mountaineer —Loch Arkaig and Loch Morar— Arisaig to Mallaig

West from Fort William beyond the pulp mill and the locks of the Caledonian Canal runs the Mallaig railway and the 'Road to the Isles', keeping together along Loch Eil-side but parting temporarily at the head of Loch Shiel, the road keeping low, the railway line looping in a horseshoe of impressive viaduct to cross Glen Finnan, the perfect viewpoint for looking down the narrows of the loch squeezed by steep mountain slopes. Its lonely austerity is emphasized by the stone figure of a Highlander on a tall column above the marshy loch-head. The motorist can walk to it over a pavement of sleepers, and climb the turret to look more closely at the figure.

The Ordnance Survey map shows it as Prince Charlie's Monument. It is more than that. Certainly it was here the Prince landed by rowing boat at noon on 19 August 1745. But the Monument is more a memorial to the Highlanders who fought and died in that sorry campaign. The figure, which looks away from the loch to the north, was not erected until 16 years after the column had been built. There has been some argument as to whether or not the figure is meant to represent the Prince or simply a Highlander.

19   *The Caledonian canal: Loch Lochy where the Ben Nevis and Grey Corries mountain range form a line of summits rising to 4,300 feet above the canal*

20   *New dwellings below Ben Nevis. From Banavie, looking over the crook of Loch Eil, to Glen Nevis*

The Rev. Angus McLean, parish minister of the time, wrote in 1838, in the *New Statistical Account of Scotland* that Angus MacDonald 'erected on the summit a statue of the Prince'. A priest of Moidart has written virtually the same story, so we can take it that the Highlanders' Monument built in 1815 is surmounted by a figure purporting to be the Prince, the complete monument dating to 1831, with Alexander MacDonald of Glenaladale building the first part, and Angus MacDonald, second successor of Alexander, adding the statue.

What kind of man was Bonnie Prince Charlie? I see him as a rangy-looking character, tall, red-haired, with a long stride and an agreeable expression which established a quick rapport with ordinary people. He was at his best in situations of discomfort, facing danger, hunger, cold, fatigue and capture. The happiest days of his life were surely the five months after Culloden, when he was the fox and Cumberland's forces, with the patrolling Royal Navy, were the pack, tracing an illusory scent to far St Kilda, and leaving a clear Arisaig coast when it was most needed by the Culloden refugees.

Standing with my back to the Monument I followed the direction of the stone figure's eyes to the top of Fraoch Bheinn and thought of the Prince lying up there, on 18 July 1746, looking down from 2,400 ft to the exact spot where the clans had rallied and marched behind him as a Highland army just eleven months before. Where were these brave men now? Dead, maimed, in prison, or even on the run like himself and his three staunch companions. These three were Glenaladale, his brother, and young John MacDonald of Borradale.

They lay on top of Fraoch Bheinn as the enemy closed in. The whole of Clanranald's country was in a stir. Ships of war were landing troops at Arisaig, along Loch Nevis and at Loch Hourn. Clansmen too were on the move, herding their cattle away from other troops marching in from the garrisons in the Great Glen by Loch Garry and Loch Arkaig.

The besieged party on top of the mountain could do nothing but wait for a guide to lead them through the mountains stretching north—well named 'The Rough Bounds'. The man they needed was Donald Cameron of Glen Pean, who had sheltered the Prince and given him curds and butter three months before, after his hard ride from the battlefield of Culloden to Loch Arkaig.

They waited until it was dangerous to wait any longer. The

21   *Atlantic breakers crash on Ardnamurchan Point*

22   *Fishing boats are the main users of the Caledonian Canal between the Moray Firth and Loch Linnhe. Pulp mill on left*

Redcoats were beginning to search the hill, so the four men crept off the summit back into the Braes of Morar to begin climbing into a lonely corrie. An amazing coincidence was to aid them that night. To avoid the obvious pass over Streap they chose a remoter way, and in the darkness of that corrie met the man they were looking for on his way to meet them.

The whole enterprise was unfortunate and disastrous for the Highlands, but the personal luck of the Prince always held when he needed it most. Charlie, when he took to the heather after Culloden, was to find the kind of company that ever afterwards made his tribulations seem a pleasure. If life had taught him any truth, it was that the risk of death with comrades true as steel is infinitely preferable to the sloth and safety of an aristocratic court.

He drank delight of adventures which were more in the nature of mountaineering than war. He tasted the joy of moving fast and far with resourceful men who were masters of their environment, peasants like Donald Cameron and outlaws like the famous band of Glen Moriston men who had sworn to carry on the war as long as there was life in them.

Donald showed his mettle at once, leading them in darkness to a recess of Sgor Thuilm at 3,000 ft, assuring them they would be safe, since he had watched the Redcoats searching this hill a few hours before. Lying up all next day, they could look down on the enemy camp at Kinlocharkaig. In every direction there were companies of searching soldiers. Only desperate men would have had the heart to brave that cordon. The hope that buoyed them was a French ship, reported to be waiting at Poolewe.

To walk there meant crossing the bristly backbone of the Western Highlands—not only the backbone, but delving between the ribs as well, into arteries and weird veins, where drainage channels end in drowned valleys like Loch Hourn and Loch Nevis.

Even today the roadmaker has not come to terms with Knoydart. It is impossible to drive through the peninsula. Only one road penetrates to the western sea coast from the east, by Invergarry and Loch Quoich to the flats of Kinloch Hourn. There is an easier penetration by sea, from Mallaig by daily mail boat to Inverie on Loch Nevis. Good paths traverse in from there, to Barrisdale and Loch Quoich, though much of the latter path is submerged now.

The Prince as a Mountaineer

The Prince's party were crossing the difficult grain of the country in the dark, dipping into Glen Pean, then climbing over a ridge to descend into Glen Dessary, creeping past lazybed cultivation and clansmen's houses. The ruins and fields are still there, even at 1,000 ft on the knolls above the lochans of the pass. Donald Cameron led his party over the shoulder of Sgor nan Coireachan into the shelter of Coire nan Gall. Then he went away foraging for food and brought back 'two small cheeses' plus the information that the troops were searching very close.

They could do nothing but wait for dusk, descend into the dangerously narrow glen beneath them, then climb the 2,000-ft slopes of Druim a' Chosaidh above. Darkness was their ally and their enemy. The flicker of fires and the sound of voices warned them to steer east by Meall an Spardain, and other fires in the new glen opening below showed them where not to descend.

In the pitch blackness their problem was to get out of this hotbed of troops by morning, without falling over a cliff. It was here the Prince nearly lost his life, following Donald Cameron, who warned him of the need for care on slippery vegetation above a considerable drop. In the slide his legs got entangled in a small tree just long enough for the others following to grab him before he could fall further.

It was lucky for them that heavy clouds obscured the moon, for in Glen Cosaidh they were now among enemy troops, and breaths must have been held as they skulked across Sron Lice na Fearna to the main chain of sentry posts stretching from Kinloch Hourn to Glen Garry.

If they could break this they were through, and they did it by slipping between sentries about a mile and a half from the head of the sea loch. They found cover none too soon, for while lying up for the day among the birches they could see soldiers searching for them. Darkness saw them moving north again, over the hills into Glen Shiel to shelter under a boulder at daybreak.

Food was their immediate requirement. They got cheese, butter, and milk. Also bad news. The ship waiting at Poolewe had sailed for France. Where now? Safer to go on than turn back, if they could find a guide who knew the country. A Glen Garry man took them in charge, eastward up the 3,600-ft peak of Sgurr nan Conbhairean to crouch for the night against an inadequate rock, while the rain and mist soaked them to the skin.

Not much of a guide you might think. But he knew what he was doing, for up there in a fine cave lived eight robbers who immediately pledged themselves to the Prince's service, gave him the cave, and appointed themselves his bodyguard. These Glen Moriston men, now immortalized, set out to fatten the Prince, bringing him whisky, mutton, cheese, butter, deer and an ox. He rested for a week near the 3,000-ft level, the whole party moving north on 1 August, two of them going ahead to Poolewe to bring back the latest news about French ships.

Note that somebody always does the dirty work. The two runners have to get themselves to the head of Loch Maree and return to the rendezvous in Glen Cannich, a long cross-country stint. And while the 26-year-old Prince waits, others of his party are out foraging for food. When I was the Prince's age I dismissed him as a nonentity. I gave credit to his companions, not to him.

I see it rather differently now. The prince was a package being pushed around, made to night-march, lie up all day, who, however tired or hungry he might feel, had to trail behind those who led him. His was a test of mental and physical stamina and he rose to it well. Anyone who has been caught out in the dark on a mountain knows how very much more tiring and nerve-racking everything is. You put your foot in holes; you slip off rocks. It is hard to cross burns and rivers. Bogs seem to be everywhere, because you cannot see to select the dry ground. A mile at night is worth three by day. Add to that exposure to wind and rain by day as well as night and you will realize that the enemy was more than mere Redcoats.

In Glen Cannich he got news that the French ship had sailed and that he would have to turn about and walk back through the hills to Locheil's country. The party of ten started their return march, feeling less danger of capture now because the troops had withdrawn to Fort Augustus. But the soldiers had left an empty land cleared of people and devoid of food. At Loch Arkaig their hunger was acute until one of the Glen Moriston men shot a stag.

The fleshpots were not so far away—no farther than 30 miles eastwards—in Cluny's Cage on Ben Alder, a two-storied shelter overlooking Loch Ericht. Locheil and Cluny MacPherson were there, and the Prince ate like a king and was treated like one, with a soft, dry couch to lie on, servants and sentries to watch over him, shoes on his feet and a new coat on his back.

The good days and convivial nights ended on 13 September, when news of a French ship in Loch nan Uamh set him moving at one in the morning. Once again the route lay by Loch Arkaig, this time by the south side and through the familiar hills to Borradale. How he must have hoped he would never have to cross that way again.

And probably the Redcoats thought the same as they marched out of the hated hills, back to Inverness and Fort Augustus. They too had been out since April, chasing from Culloden to the Outer Hebrides, tossed about in boats, dumped on lonely coasts and left in God-forsaken wildernesses to search misty mountains that were not even mapped.

The Prince sailed away on 20 September but left behind him the only part of his life that mattered. For ever afterwards he looked back in anger at the might-have-been of his world of fantasy, convinced that if this or that had not happened the Stuart cause would have been victorious.

Only one thing remained very real to him, however, and that was the selfless loyalty of the ordinary Highlanders, men like Donald Cameron and the Glen Moriston men, Flora Macdonald, and all the other chance folk who took risks for him. The dreamer of dreams knew reality when he met it in such obvious form. If his imagination had matched his physique, Scotland might be a different country today. He did not seem to realize the consequences for the Highlanders and the Highlands should his army be cut to ribbons. Completely lacking understanding about the Highlands, he took everything he saw around him for granted.

Things went too well for him. True he had trouble with the chiefs; he knew they were jealous, proud men, but they always stood by him. He had reason to live in the present and not worry about the future; his volunteer army, fighting by instinct rather than leadership, never lost a battle until Culloden. And that failure must lie squarely on the Prince, who should have withdrawn his unprepared men, when the chance to take the enemy by surprise was lost. But his vanity was aroused. He was the son of a king determined to fight another son of a king, William Augustus, Duke of Cumberland. And his adjutant-general, O'Sullivan, perhaps the worst quartermaster in history, chose Culloden Moor for the stand.

The Prince was the lucky one. He escaped. His army did not. The rape of the Highlands by Cumberland was calculated to ensure that a fifth column would never again arise to menace the safety of England. The word 'atrocity' had little political meaning until the Massacre of Glencoe, 54 years earlier, when the quibble over the oath of allegiance was taken as an excuse for foul murder. The infamous massacre was nothing compared with the outrage of Cumberland's crimes.

These were the events which led to the final destruction of the clan system, which was an anachronism in an increasingly organized political age, because the people gave their allegiance to their chiefs rather than to society. A clan was a tribe which owned tribal land, and all rights were common rights. But it is important to remember that the clan system was the opposite of feudalism.

Feudalism did not arrive in the Western Highlands until the clan lands were carved into private estates. Knoydart was inhabited entirely by gamekeepers when I went there first, the last of its natives having been cleared from their crofts in 1853. The Highlands I was born into was one where the absentee landlord was king, and woe betide any gamekeeper who sheltered any passing traveller or allowed him to put up a tent. The pastures were strictly for deer or sheep, and in some parts there is little sign of any change of attitude.

One walk I must recommend is from the west end of Loch Arkaig by Glen Pean to Loch Morar where the motor run is exciting. Swinging away from the Commando Monument above Spean Bridge you cross the Caledonian Canal to follow the wooded Loch Lochy shore. An interesting alternative is by Banavie on the line of the old Caledonian railway for a look at the steps of Neptune's Staircase, a virtual ladder of locks to enable passage of the canal. Fully mechanized now, it takes a ship just over an hour to surmount this obstacle as against over two hours by the old 'stick and chain' method. Boats up to 160 ft by 36 ft can be taken, and the 60-mile passage from sea to sea takes 10–11 hours. Pulp ships and pleasure craft are important sources of revenue.

The view from Loch Lochy, where you turn off for Loch Arkaig, is perhaps the best on the canal. The clachan of houses is Bunarkaig on a wide bay fronting the Ben Nevis massif. You look right into the great mass of its cliffs and ridges and leftward to the continuing summits of the Grey Corries. From this position at a mere 93 ft above sea level they are impressive, and truly alpine when spring has arrived down here but it is still icy winter up there.

This is Cameron country, and the present Locheil lives above the short Arkaig River. The house is on the site of the original home destroyed by Cumberland for Locheil's part in the Rising. And Locheil's was a big part, for he was the first to join the Prince at Glenfinnan, bagpipes playing, at the head of over 700 men. He rose, though he knew in his heart that nothing good could come of the enterprise. He went into exile with the Prince and died in France.

But 40 years later the Highlands had been pacified. The Government felt confident. The forfeited estates were offered back to the rebels, with the difference that the chiefs had the title of the land. Many abused their trust and evicted the clansfolk to get higher rents from Lowland flockmasters. Unfortunately the Camerons are not exempt from blame here in the nineteenth century when Loch Arkaigside and Glen Dessary were cleared.

Campers may purchase a permit at the cottage marking entrance to the 'Dark Mile', so called because its canopy of trees cuts out the light from the sky in the short drive to Loch Arkaig. Difficult driving begins just past the big waterfall as you join the loch for twelve miles of single-track blind bumps and tortuous bends. Locheil manages his land in a multi-purpose way, as sheep farm, deer forest and coniferous woodland, allowing recreational facilities in little numbered camp sites favoured by caravanners and fishermen after the big trout in the loch. The skeletal pines of the south shore are remnants of the Caledonian forest which Commandos set alight during the war.

The road ends beside a little school and the farm of Strathan. The 'Rough Bounds' lie ahead. Glenfinnan is only nine miles away between the two shapely peaks of Streap and Sgor Thuilm. Loch Hourn lies behind a wall of bristling mountains. A good path leads through Glen Dessary to Loch Nevis. But it was to Loch Morar by Glen Pean the Prince went from Kinlocharkaig after his hard ride from Culloden and overnight rest. The ruins of a house at Kinlocharkaig are almost certainly the ruins of Donald Cameron's house.

Here on the night of 17 April Donald rose from his bed at the sound of horses and voices. The travellers were the Prince and his party, bearing bad news of the battle: defeat at Culloden the day before, and

Locheil shot through the legs, but rescued by Camerons of the clan. Now Donald was to entertain Charlie himself, tired out and hungry. All next day the fugitives lay up, anxiously waiting for news, then at 5 p.m. set off down Glen Pean.

Much has been written about the physical toughness of Bonnie Prince Charlie. The walk down Glen Pean over the 500-ft pass to Loch Morar and along to Meoble is said to have brought him near the end of his tether. No doubt this is because of what he had been through, for a strong walker will have no difficulty in making the return journey to Loch Morar in a day.

The least interesting part is the beginning where the glen is broad and soggy, with stepping stones leading across the river to a ruined settlement whose lazybed cultivation still shows like projecting ribs in the bracken. But in three miles or so the mountains begin to close in on you, until at the Lochan Leum an-t-Sagairt you are in a miniature Glen Coe, with birch woods hanging on crags above you and a wild-looking ravine beyond.

The route ahead is not obvious from here. The way lies along the south side, so look out for a cairn marking a rising sheep track, winding in and out of gullies and descending again to the floor of a narrowing glen. This is the true pass, with the east-flowing stream no more than a rivulet disappearing snake-like among a litter of gigantic boulders.

This is marked on the map 'Coir' a' Bheigh', and is the wildest surprise of Glen Pean, for you are now in a defile of tangled rocks cradling a minute lochan. Rock walls hem you in, and just over the crest you get your first view of Loch Morar. The path is good and the descent is easy, ending at an empty house called Oban on the south shore, but continuing on along the north shore for the whole length of the loch. From Loch Arkaig I did the return journey comfortably in ten hours' walking, with frequent steps to enjoy the country.

When Charlie did the walk he went along the south shore a few miles to reach Meoble where he stayed the night 'in a small sheal house near a wood'. I went to this attractive spot a different way, by Glen Beasdale from Loch nan Uamh so as to follow the last part of Charlie's route. This fine glen of natural oaks gives out on rough moor with small lochans out of which issues a stream flowing to the green parks and woods of a clachan of houses.

Meoble, I discovered, belongs to the Ferranti Estate and is run as a farm and deer forest, with a community of eight including a schoolteacher whose class is supplemented by children from four miles further down the loch. For getting about their four miles of private road they had a Land Rover, and for maintaining contact with the outside world there was a powerful motor launch. The estate marches with Locheil's at Glen Pean.

For the return trip I took the direct route south on a path which climbs steeply for a thousand feet to cross a ridge and drop by the Allt na Criche to the Dubh Loch a mile from Lochailort. Thumbing a lift on a fish lorry I was soon back at my car after a really interesting day among red deer, golden eagles and black-throated divers.

An easier way of seeing Loch Morar is from the Mallaig road at Morar, following the narrow driving road on its north side as far as you can go to Bracarina. Walkers will find a delightful path from here, climbing in three miles to a vantage point overlooking Loch Nevis to the north and Loch Morar to the south. The path goes on to Easter Stoul, a remote crofting hamlet facing the 'Rough Bounds'. The dominant peak is the point of Sgor na Ciche, 3,410 ft, one of the finest viewpoints in Scotland, easily climbable from Glen Dessary.

Loch Morar, speckled with scrubby islands at its western end and narrowing as it goes eastward in the 11½ miles of its length, is in a class by itself, for it is the deepest loch in Scotland at 1,077 ft and boatmen have had encounters with a 'monster' said to lurk there. It should be mentioned perhaps that Loch Ness, with its better known monster, is the second deepest loch in Scotland at 754 ft, and both are not very far above the level of the sea, Ness at 53 ft, Morar at 30 ft.

The 'Rough Bounds' owe their roughness to extreme glaciation, as the peaks emerged from an ice-cap, and ancient valley systems were dredged deeper by moving ice-streams. Loch Morar is a rock basin dug out by a 4,000-ft bulldozer of ice. The same applies to Loch Nevis and Loch Hourn, though they have been invaded by the sea, and it should be noticed that both have inner fjords where the wide sea lochs narrow from mouths to drowned valleys.

Loch Morar is harnessed for hydro-electric power now, where the river emerges from its western end, and the scrubby islands bearing natural trees are worthy of attention. It was on one of them that Lord Lovat of the '45 was captured, plucked from his hiding place in a hollow tree and taken to London to be executed.

The white sands of Morar and Arisaig have become justifiably famous, particularly among campers and caravanners on a greensward stretching from the roadside to the sea. Even on a wet day there is a lightness and brightness in the sudden opening of the Atlantic, spattered with magical islands, the notch of Eigg and the thrusting peaks of Rhum, and the Cuillin of Skye just across the water. The view from the train as it turns the corner past Loch nan Uamh is the best manifestation of that view. But first we should look at Loch nan Uamh.

This is where Charlie was making for when he rode from Culloden and walked by Glen Pean and Meoble to Borradale House. It was here the Prince first set foot on the Scottish mainland; it was here, on 19 August 1745, that the Highland chiefs tried to dissuade him from his mad fantasy of conquering Britain; and it was here on 20 April 1746, he met his staff officers who had survived Culloden. They foregathered at Borradale House, burned down later by Cumberland, but the plain square building is still spoken of as the house where the Prince stayed, and is part of a farm in a vital setting of brown hills, suddenly smoothing to a tableland of greensward sheltered by oakwoods and ending in a white curve of bay.

The Prince's Cave, where he stayed at a later stage in the manhunt, is fairly close to the house but you would miss it unless you were looking for a hole among boulders, a mere vent 30 ft up on a cliff, descending into darkness. I found it a delightful surprise, squeezing through a manhole into a dark vault with wet sides, which gradually became bone-dry where it flattened into a narrow chamber that could accommodate half-a-dozen or more men. It is a comfortable cave, sheltered from every wind, and a party sitting at the entrance could observe without being seen. It can be reached from Drumdarroch as well as from Borradale, and it lies fairly close to the gate where the drive-way from the latter house ends in a field.

Round a headland from it, carved out of the rock, is a natural deep-water jetty, the one the Prince sailed from, most probably, on the night of 26 April against the advice of the old boatman, Donald MacLeod of Skye, who forecast a storm and wanted to wait. But the Prince, always a powerful persuader of other men, got his way in the face of wisdom, and was hardly out of the Sound of Arisaig before he was asking the impossible, to be set ashore again.

Well, he raised the standard against advice; he forced the issue of
Culloden against advice; and now, against advice, he was on the sea
in an eight-oared boat, heading out into the Atlantic, into blackness,
on a night that got worse and worse as waves broke over them, the
wind becoming a gale, and rain adding to the misery of seasickness.

Without compass, and with bowsprit broken, they could have been
wrecked on Skye or driven far west of the Long Island. But again his
luck held. At dawn they saw land, and were able to pull in at Rossinish
in Benbecula, close to a deserted hut which must have seemed like a
palace, with wood for a fire and shelter from the raw wind which was
still blowing.

The object of their dangerous journey was to try to get a vessel to
France. If they had waited only a day or two longer at Borradale
a vessel would have come to them—two vessels, in fact, the *Bellona*
and the *Mars*, bringing muskets, ammunition, and 36,000 *louis d'or*
from the King of France.

I tried to picture the scene as I sat by the jetty on Loch nan Uamh,
the faces of the war-scarred Jacobite leaders, peering from cover at
the two ships under sail, thinking them English naval vessels come to
harry them, then with relief realizing that the flags were French,
and rushing down to them with a cheer.

But a shock was coming when, in the early morning, the Jacobites
waiting on the shore saw three more ships under sail rounding the bay,
and they were not French. They were the English frigates *Greyhound*,
Baltimore and *Terror*, down from Fort William, closing for a gun
battle—recoiling cannon, bursts of smoke, men falling dead, the
English ships in full sail trying to blow up the ships at anchor, while all
the time the Jacobite shore party struggle to unload casks of money and
brandy for the three hours that the battle lasts, until the English
frigates hoist sail and break off the engagement, leaving the French
victorious.

Into exile on the *Bellona* and *Mars* sailed many Jacobites, harbouring
hard thoughts about the Prince who had sailed west only a few days
before. Meantime there was loot for those who stayed at Borradale,
and before some of the gold had been taken to Loch Arkaig and
dumped, nobody knows where, robbery had been done. Young
Barrisdale and his clansmen, laden with money and casks of brandy,

made off, while Murray of Broughton is reviled for not going with the Jacobites to France, but remaining to turn traitor and loot the treasure.

Yes, a quiet place Borradale, full of the ghosts of history, but so is this whole coast.

The Prince had lost his chance of easy escape to France by being in too big a hurry to get away from Borradale. He was in an even bigger hurry to get back to it on 5 July, after two months of boats and bothies, tramping over the hills of Harris, Uist and Skye, as he fled from naval frigates or dodged searching troops. But always when things seemed most hopeless, some ordinary person, usually a non-Jacobite, would risk everything for him spurning a reward of £30,000. There are different kinds of nobility. A MacIain sheltered the Prince when he could have betrayed him. Yet the man was so poor that he stole a cow and hanged for it.

The day-to-day life of unexpected happenings seemed to suit the Prince's temperament. In an alarm he was cool; in an excursion he was strong. He would share the cooking with Ned Burke, mixing meal with brains of cow to make his own special bannock, or cook fish on a little island on Loch Shell, Lewis, before rowing to Loch Maddy, then to Benbecula for the crossing to Skye with Flora MacDonald. The episode with Flora is the best-known story in the campaign, when he dressed up as a woman to pass himself off as Betty Burke, maid-servant to the valiant Flora.

Lowlanders did not give much for the scenery of the Highlands in 1745. Like the Alps of Switzerland, the country was regarded as rude, barbaric, savage, ugly, fearsome, gloomy, or terrible. In these hills travelling was dangerous and life a primitive struggle for survival, where large families lived in single rooms of thatched roofs and more time was spent on war and games than on work. By eighteenth-century standards it was a tribal and inefficient society and Lowlanders held the Highlanders in contempt.

Yet in 1773 when Dr Samuel Johnson was talked into visiting the Highlands and Islands by Boswell, this is what he wrote:

There was perhaps never any change of national manners so quick, so great, and so general, as that which has operated in the Highlands by the last conquest and the subsequent laws. We came hither too late to see what we expected—a people of peculiar appearance, and a system of antiquated life. The clans retain little now of their original character: their ferocity of temper is softened, their military ardour is extinguished, their dignity of independence is depressed, their contempt of government subdued, and their reverence for their chiefs abated. Of what they had before the late conquest of their country there remains only their language and their poverty.

I like the doctor's account of his stay at Lochbuie in Mull—'where we found a true Highland laird, rough and haughty, and tenacious of his dignity; who, hearing my name, inquired whether I was of the Johnstones of Glencoe or of Ardnamurchan'. From that statement it becomes clear that the MacIains translated their name into literal English, the sons of John, though the spelling should be John*son* and not John*stone*. The first chief was Iain Og nan Fraoch, which in English is 'Young John of the Heather'. He dates back to the fourteenth century and all the MacIain chiefs descend from him.

Had Johnson lived another 50 years and travelled the Highlands and Islands again, he would have seen real poverty and unrelieved congestion, the result of a population explosion following the ending of clan warfare, together with an economy built up on the cultivation of small patches of potatoes and the burning of seaweed for kelp. The new owners of the land were doing well from rents until the price for kelp fell from £20 a ton in 1808 to £3 a ton in 1830. Then came the potato famine in 1840 and destitution reached new levels. There was no alternative to emigration. Together with the evictions, it meant the death of the Gaelic language.

Yet in Mallaig, back all the way to Fort William, Gaelic remained the spoken language until the coming of the railway put the emphasis on English. That 40 miles of railway which took three years to build was opened in 1901. Until then Mallaig was nothing, merely a point of land and a house or two, thatch-roofed. Local fishermen sold their catch from the net to waiting schooners which took it to Glasgow. My informant was John MacDougall from Sandaig across Loch Nevis. In these days the Mallaig folk had to cross the water to Mass in his township chapel. And on the occasion of the arrival of the first train, John sat on top of the hill watching a flotilla of four or five boats steaming to meet it.

Mallaig owes its present pier and breakwater to the railway, the Government of the time contributing £30,000 towards its cost in the hope that crofting and fishing would benefit. The railways did have a profound effect on the fisheries, by bringing the railhead to the fishing grounds. Nowadays there is no fish going by rail. The catches of this important market go by lorry, and the only freight that brings a stir to the line is the arrival of the summer tourists. The future of the line is uncertain, and it will be a sad loss if it goes.

In a world of change it preserves an air of timeless peace. A lone traveller is seldom lonely for long, and in its carriages I have heard more good talk than almost anywhere else in the world. And from its staff I have had nothing but kindness, except once when at midnight I stole into a railway carriage laid-up in a siding and was caught in the morning lying full-stretch in my sleeping bag. The man's anger was not so much at my taking liberties with railway stock as for covering the upholstery with eiderdown feathers from my leaking bag.

In Mallaig station there is a Gaelic notice which translates 'Each home in this hospitable place is giving you a hearty welcome'. I have found it to be true.

CHAPTER SEVEN

Knoydart, Skye and Raasay

Loch Hourn and Arnisdale—Gavin Maxwell's Camusfearna—Inverie on Loch Nevis— Skye—Raasay

The motorist who has exhausted Mallaig must make the crossing of the Sound of Sleat to Armadale if he wants to keep going north and remain at the wheel. The enchantment of Skye may contain him, or he may merely use its tail-end as a stepping stone to cross back to the mainland at the first opportunity. The two ferry points are at Kyleakin for Kyle of Lochalsh, and at Kylerhea for Glenelg. I recommend the latter if you would see some more of Knoydart.

From Glenelg to Arnisdale by ten miles of winding switchback road is a must for any collector of difficult roads. It is without doubt the loneliest approach to any village in Scotland. The route becomes exciting as the shoulder of Ben Screel closes in, and you begin to feel yourself edging along between the mountain and the sea, on a narrower ledge than you would wish, when any moment something might appear round the bend in front.

Maybe you can enjoy the big-scale scenery if you are a passenger. As a driver it is impossible, especially at the 1 in 5 drop from hill to village at the end. The number of houses comes as a surprise, and the small number of permanent residents as a shock. Arnisdale is really two hamlets, Camus Ban above the neat horseshoe of the bay, and Corran, a mile distant across the Arnisdale River. Between the two villages is the 'Big House', built by the father of Ian Fleming, writer of James Bond thrillers.

Arnisdale is a radiant place when the sun shines, in a setting of mountains, river, glen and sea loch. Over the Sound of Sleat is the jagged array of the Cuillin, and just across the water are the big hills of Knoydart above Barrisdale. On my first visit here I walked through the hills from Loch Quoich and climbed Ladhar Bheinn from Barrisdale, the most westerly peak over 3,000 ft on the Scottish mainland.

I had climbed its neighbours first, Meall Buidhe and Luinne Bheinn, so the sun was westering as I topped the twin buttresses and looked on a world ablaze from Ardnamurchan to Torridon, and from Skye to the Outer Hebrides. What a position from which to enjoy the Sound of Sleat, like a molten river between Skye just across the water, and the wriggling headlands forming the mouths of the big sea lochs.

On my last visit in 1971 I stayed in Arnisdale, and learned a few things about the state of the village. The population of the two villages was 51, I was told, and of 31 houses, only 21 were permanently occupied. The others are let out as holiday homes. That ratio of occupied houses was high, I realized, when I heard there are only six jobs available for the menfolk, three in forestry and three on the estate.

George MacDougall, aged 84, was born here, but spent most of his life in Glasgow. 'I would never have left if I could have got 3s (15p) a day, which was the standard wage of that time, but there was no steady work. I used to go away in the spring with the other young men and get jobs on the roads or on construction schemes, and come back again for the herring fishing. I've worked as a ghillie and a shepherd—yes, even since coming back after 40 years in Glasgow.

'What we need is a better road or Arnisdale is finished. There's not even a school here nowadays. The five children have to travel every day to the primary school in Glenelg. Two older ones have to board at Inverness and Plockton. We need an outlet to the outside world through Glen Arnisdale to Kinloch Hourn. It's much less in distance than from Glenelg to here.'

George was an enthusiast for Arnisdale, I could see. 'There's no more beautiful place in the West. It's only the lack of a through road that's stopping people coming. And the road would be handy, too, for the Skye folk, who would be able to get out to the Great Glen by coming this way.' Such a road would come out at Invergarry. But the most pressing need on my visit was an improvement to the Glenelg road, which was so bad that the Forestry Commission had given up trying to get their timber to the pulp mill.

23 *Loch Nevis from Sgurr na Ciche, with the Isle of Eigg seen across the sea*

Yet older people like George MacDougall can remember boyhood days when Loch Hourn was a busy place, so thronged with herring boats that it was possible to use them as stepping stones between north and south shore. The long row of dry-stone huts just south of Corran village is where the fisherfolk stowed their gear. A similar row behind the village, with numbers on the doors, provided each crofter with a byre for his cow. Today there are ten crofts, neatly kept and fenced.

One pilgrimage I felt we had to make when we were there was to Camusfearna, where Gavin Maxwell wrote *Ring of Bright Water*. To get there we motored half way back to Glenelg and left the car at the only house on the roadside. Here we were told: 'Go through the white gate immediately opposite and follow the track down through the forest. There is no house there now. Gavin Maxwell's ashes are buried under a slab of rock where the house used to stand.'

It was raining as we went down, over undulating ground at first, which gradually steepened and the path became rocky. Nothing to see until we were over the crest of the bluff, then below us was a green meadow, grey sea and beyond it the hills of Skye, dimmed by sweeping showers. It was the first time we had seen the place of which Maxwell had written: 'Nowhere in all the West Highlands and Islands have I seen a place of so intense or varied beauty in so small a compass.'

I thought of him arriving here, with a rucksack on his back, and seeing before him a white two-storied house, of turning the key in the lock, lighting the primus and throwing his sleeping bag and utensils down. The man who had been trying to earn his living as a portrait painter had arrived at the crossroads of his life almost by chance. An Oxford friend who owned the house had offered it to him. As he wrote in *Ring of Bright Water*: 'This place has been my home now for ten years and more, and wherever the changes of my life may lead me in the future, it will remain my spiritual home until I die . . ..'

Down past the waterfall and we stood by the fragment of pink rock under which his ashes lie. I thought of the crystal vision that these early years had given him, and of how marvellously he had communicated it in his writing, when he lived simply and close to nature, delighting in the otters and the whole gamut of wild life in front of him.

I walked over to the waterfall of which he wrote: 'It is the waterfall, rather than the house, that has always seemed to me the soul of

Camusfearna, and if there is anywhere in the world to which some part of me may return when I am dead it will be there.'

In *Raven Seek Thy Brother* he shows how the purity of the dream came to its end, as he built a road to the house, disfigured the water-fall 'by black alcathene piping that carried water to the house and to the otters' enclosures', and found the natural world steadily receding under paper and telephone work. Camusfearna with a staff of employees, powerboats, Land Rovers, cars, electricity and supply problems, had become a little empire whose upkeep alone was costing £7,000 a year.

I went to the rowan tree and looked at the burial cairn of Edal, the otter who had perished in the fire which had left nothing but a shell of a house in January 1968. I thought of what Maxwell had written: 'Tonight at the last sentence of a dream I stand in thought before the Camusfearna door. Someone, someday, perhaps, may build again on that site, but there is much that cannot even be rebuilt.'

Surely no man in 19 years of living here will ever again know such deep joy, and poignant sorrow and pain, or produce so much that answers to the name of literature. When the simplicity went out of Camusfearna the idyll died; Maxwell's private life went wrong and his privacy was invaded. Animal and human relations became painful. Ironically, it was his astonishing financial success in writing about the otters he loved which set in train the events leading to disenchantment and near despair.

The magical rowan remains. A curse upon Maxwell was fulfilled. The house has vanished even more completely than the former township of 200 people who scraped a living here until the nineteenth century when they were evicted with the Arnisdale crofters. The rickles of stones tell one sad tale, and the cairn of stones to Edal tells another. But the things of everlasting value are the books about otters and a man who loved them.

You will look in vain for the name Camusfearna on any map. Maxwell used it in order to disguise its location. The bay with the little islands is called Sandaig on the map, not to be confused with another Sandaig further down the Sound of Sleat on the upper jaw of Loch Nevis. That other Sandaig is equal in charm, but is inaccessible except by walking. The best way to it is from Mallaig, by daily mail boat from Mallaig to Inverie, then by the coast road. Anyone wishing

to 'get-away-from-it-all' should try for accommodation at Inverie.
A bicycle is useful.

But let's hear something of the place from another MacDougall, my
old friend John, who was born in Sandaig in 1886. 'There was no
mail boat from Mallaig in my early days. The letters went to Isle-
oronsay in Skye and came to Airor by boat. And from there they were
taken by pony to Inverie. MacBrayne's boat, the *Claymore*, brought
the provisions twice a week from Glasgow and dumped them at
Inverie. You took them home yourself.'

'By horse?' I queried.

'I was the horse. There was four occupied houses in Sandaig then,
and nine families in Airor. Now there's nobody in Sandaig and only
two crofters at the end of the tarred road to Airor. I left Knoydart
because my own house was so bad. They had been promising to do
something about it for 20 years. There was not even a wood lining in
it. The walls were thick with verdigris. And the highest wage I ever
got was £12 the half-year. I was 37 when I left.'

John's father came to Knoydart as a shepherd, and John followed
on as his successor, working as a ghillie in the deer-stalking season when
he was a lad, and always keeping the ten acres of croft going. 'You
never knew what a holiday was because every day was a holiday. Yes,
I was happy in Knoydart.'

Mrs Nellie Woodhall, née Huggins, told me some more about
Knoydart. A contemporary of John, her father was head gardener on
the estate. 'When my father first came to Knoydart it was owned by
a Mr John Baird, who was, I believe, a mine owner in Ayrshire. He
built the cottages in Strath near Inverie pier on the pattern of 'Miners'
Rows'—one room and a cupboard-like annexe, which only just held
a bed. Here large families ate, slept, lived and died. One early
recollection of mine is a school friend telling me when her father died,
his body had to be placed on the floor so that the family could go to bed.

'Successive landlords improved things in many ways, though
visitors were not encouraged. The small inn was not allowed to take
anyone. Knoydart was a happy place—dances, fun at Hallowe'en,
and New Year ceilidhs. We made our own fun.

'Except for the short season when the laird and his family were in
residence for shooting and stalking we had complete freedom, and
what a happy childhood I remember. The estate then was largely

self-supporting, with home farm, sawmill, masons, and foresters. I am saddened to hear recently from a friend that the gardens and woods my father planted and tended for 48 years are now a wilderness or cut down.

'Airor I remember as a crofting community of several families. For a short time I taught in the small school. Though for the past 50 years I have lived in England, my heart remains in Knoydart. . . .'

One of the finest walks in the whole of the Western Highlands is, in my view, the path from Inverie over a low pass into Gleann na Guiserein, to follow the coast of the Sound of Sleat to Airor, then by road back to Inverie. The walking is easy and the circular tour is not more than 15 miles.

On the way through the glen and along the shore you will see innumerable ruins and cultivation patches. Relics of ancient history? Not really. Mrs MacDonell, wife of the sixteenth Chief, cleared the last 400 unwanted people in 1853. And she travelled up from Edinburgh to supervise the burning of the houses of those who refused to go. The *Sillery*—a Government ship—stood by to take them to America whenever they were persuaded to go. Those who stayed had to seek shelter in caves.

Why did Mrs MacDonell do it? Did she take the view that by evicting her people and sending them to the New World she was giving a fresh start to deserving people with brains, so that they could use them to make America a better place? Or did she do it so that she could sell Knoydart at a better price once the crofters were out of it? Remember that half-a-dozen years before her evictions there was potato blight and famine which forced many to emigrate. Knoydart was bought by a Lowland industrialist, and there is no doubt at all that Mrs Josephine MacDonnell got a good price for it. The evictions were carried out just a year after the Chief had been buried in Inverie.

Ever since then visitors to Knoydart have not been encouraged. This is the background to the story of the Seven Men of Knoydart who on a November day in 1948 moved in on the laird's land and began making crofts for themselves. One of them was John MacDougall's son, and like the others he was interdicted, and that was the end of the land-hungry men of Knoydart. The law was the law, and the landlord had it on his side.

A *Ballad of the Men of Knoydart* was composed by one, Seumas **Mor**, and sung to the tune of *Johnstone's Motor Car*. Here is a sample of it:

'Twas down by the farm of Scottas, Lord Brocket walked one day,
And he saw a sight that worried him, far more than he could say,
For the Seven Men of Knoydart were doing what they'd planned,
They had staked their claims and were digging their drains
On Brocket's private land.

'You bloody Reds,' Lord Brocket yelled, 'Wot's this you're doing 'ere?
It doesn't pay as you'll find today to insult an English peer,
You're only Scottish half-wits, but I'll make you understand.
You Highland swine, these hills are mine! This is all
Lord Brocket's land.'

The rude answer, which I won't give here, disconcerts the Lord of the estate, who replies:

These dukes of Sutherland, were right about the Scot.
If I had my way, I'd start today, and clear the whole damn lot.

An inquiry was held, the men dispersed and, as I write this, only two of them are in Knoydart. One of them has a croft and keeps the only shop. Houses and a village hall occupy some of the debatable land today. The big green which the raiders tried to dig lies empty. Take a short walk up Glen Dulochain, up through a jungle of oaks, limes, chestnuts, spruces, pines and birches for an unusual sight—a pointed cairn shaped like a Tibetan chorten perched on a knoll—dramatic against the highest hills. It was erected to the memory of the late Lord Brocket's father. The widow of the sixteenth chief has her own memorial in the ruins of this empty land.

Now we go to Skye, the most popular of the islands, whose appeal is mainly due to the pattern of the crofting system imposed upon striking peaks, white dots of houses on pocket handkerchiefs of fields above the sea.

Stopping in Strath Suardal at the vision of haymakers dwarfed by the great wall of Blaven—3,000 ft of it—I was joined by another motorist similarly arrested. 'It reminds me of Austria,' he said. I had never thought of it that way, but I saw what he meant, for the neatly shaved squares of green with their yellow haystacks were just like alpine meadows, and the shadowy face of rock splintered by rock pinnacles could have been somewhere in Zillertal.

'I must have a chat to the crofters,' I said, hopping over a fence and climbing up to where the small figures were forking hay on the crest of a ridge. One had his shirt off, the other in white singlet gave me a cheery greeting. 'We could do with a hand to turn it before the midges come out,' he grinned.

I congratulated him on his view, which included the sea which had been hidden before. 'It's fine in weather like this when the ground's easy to work. We've had no rain for three months, so the crop is short and the hay is light. It's fine when you have someone to help you, for during the week I have to work it myself. I have to fork the hay, then climb on to the cart and spread it then go down and do the same all over again.'

The man with his back to me was a relative, giving him a Saturday afternoon. 'What about the other crofters, don't you all muck in and help each other?'

'That's a thing of the past,' he replied. 'Right enough, the four crofters who make up this township run a sheep club. We have 320 between us, but that's as far as community work goes. The reason is the other crofters are working. They are busy with other jobs during the day, so they need their spare time for their own crofts. I am the only full-time crofter, and I can only make a living off it because I am just myself. I couldn't keep a wife and family on it.'

I remarked that he must like crofting better than working at a steady job or he would be out of it by now. 'This job is steady enough,' he said. 'You can't be thinking of holidays when you depend on a croft, or be going to the pub every night. It's a luxury if you get an old cast ewe at the back-end. You get your eggs and you grow some of your food. You see my oats, potatoes and vegetables down there?'

'You make it sound pessimistic, but I think you must enjoy being your own master,' I replied.

'It takes two to manage, and I'm sure I would be better with a job, or doing what nearly everybody on Skye does now, taking in summer visitors.' But he had no thought of taking a wife and entering into the tourist business. 'Good wives are scarce. The girls nowadays are better at sitting in the cocktail bar than working.'

The Skye folk have their own brand of humour, and I could see he was weighing me up to see how I was taking this. 'Anyway you know where you are with twelve cows and twelve calves, plus your sheep on the hill, and feed to see them through the winter.'

The alternative was a job in the marble quarry near by. It produces chips and employs 20 men. One of its workers was forking hay on his croft as I passed, while alongside a transistor radio was playing loud pop music. He told me he was on his holidays and couldn't afford to go away because he had five children.

'I meant to take a long lie today, but the sunshine brought me out at my usual time. We start at 7.30 in the quarry and stop at 6.30.' He didn't think it was an unusually long day. 'The money's good. I can usually make £18–£20 a week, and there's not much wrong with that when you have a croft.'

This far south-west corner of Skye is my favourite bit, not just around Loch Slapin, but all the way from Tarskavaig, because you always have crofts in the foreground against the Cuillin across the sea. Elgol surpassed any previous view I had ever had of it on that evening of absolute perfection, its perched houses and sharply sloping fields modelled against the greatest horseshoe of precipitous peaks in Britain, even sharper and more jagged than I remembered them.

Hard to go to bed on such a night with the glow in the west still burning as the moon set over Rhum. And far behind the flash of Oig-sgeir light you could trace the outline of the Long Island, while the notches of the Cuillin pricked the sky as if cut from coal.

Such a promise of flawless weather was rare in my own experience of countless wet and windy holidays in Skye. Indeed I climbed every peak in the Cuillin before I saw the ridge clear. But I was back the next year to be washed out again. And such was the attraction of the Cuillin that as a serving soldier I travelled from Dover to Skye to spend my leaves climbing. I have lost count of my visits but the lure of this linked chain of 24 rock peaks remains.

In the morning we set off on the shore walk by Loch Scavaig to Loch Coruisk, beginning at the highest crofts and slanting down to wind in and out of gullies above the sea. The narrow footpath is good but requires care in one or two places, so make a stop if you want to look at Arctic terns, stonechats, red-throated divers or eider ducks. Then you round the big bay of Camusunary, cross a suspension bridge over the river and begin the section that leads to the 'Bad Step'.

The route now lies round the shoulder of Sgurr na Stri which becomes rockier as you go, threading rock slabs and tumbled boulders. The Bad Step is the move across a slab barring your way. It is not in the least difficult, not if you remember to keep fairly low, following an obvious crack, but making sure you break off left on another easy gangway before you get too high. The connecting gangways are much more obvious on the return journey. There is, however, an alternative to the Bad Step.

The alternative route is strongly marked in white paint. It goes up a gully and after a horizontal traverse descends again. On the day of our walk we saw people who would neither cross the Bad Step nor its alternative. They were intimidated by both routes, which is an indication that the walk is not for everybody.

Most people in fact sail to Loch Coruisk on the numerous excursions from Elgol, alighting at the Scavaig shore and scrambling up the short river to the impressive rock basin penetrating into the heart of the range. The walker with no need to return to the starting point can have fun breaking over the Cuillin by the Bealach Coire na Banadich, or to Sligachan by Druim Hain. Camping at Loch Coruisk is better than it looks. True the ground quakes, but the drier bogs between the river and the climbing hut are surprisingly good.

The traverse of the main Cuillin ridge in a single 10,000 ft rock-climbing day still eludes me after three attempts. The last one was on a May weekend from Glasgow with a Scottish Mountaineering Club party. To Mallaig by car on the Friday night, we chartered Bruce Watt's *Western Isles* to sail us to Coruisk on the Saturday morning. Lovely to sail out in our own little craft into spasms of sunshine glittering on the sea and lifting puffy cloud camps from the big hills of Knoydart.

Lots of birds on the water, rafts of guillemots and razorbills, with twists of shearwaters skimming about. Saw two great northern divers, their clean flanks as white as the new snow glistening on Sgurr nan Gillean. Rhum and Ardnamurchan Point looked very close in the sharp visibility, as we sailed under the green crofts of Elgol to Loch Scavaig, where seals lay on the rocks, not bothering to move as we chugged to the landing place.

The rush of 26 men ashore was comical to witness as groups broke off like blackcock on the lek, each looking for a territory on the quaking bog. Each was searching for a firm tump, and having found it they took firm possession by throwing down their sacks and stretching the canvas. Our own tump was beneath a big rock boss, and we soon had to turn the tent round because of wind deflections hitting the rock and gusting the stove.

Coruisk means the 'corrie of the waters' and we spent the afternoon doing a round of its shores, walking over glistening slabs and balancing on tussocks in the bogs. The acreage of rock about Loch Coruisk is relieved by a little green island in the loch, even a few trees at one place, and meadows round its headwaters. There was life too, a pair of greenshank, the loud 'kek-kek-keking' of a peregrine falcon and the sight of a golden eagle. A spurt of silver from a wren was the only bird song. We were taking our ease because we were planning a 5 a.m. start to do the whole ridge.

In fact it was 10.45 before we left, but the rain which had foiled an earlier departure was now easing off. The Cuillin were invisible in mist but we trusted it would roll away by the time we were up there. It did, dramatically, when the clouds submerged on each side of us and the rock edge of the ridge swung like a bridge in space before us. Through holes in the streaming vapour the Isle of Soay lay like a pancake 3,000 ft down, its birches showing green on dun bogs, while to the north, black fangs of peaks were materializing from the dispersing clouds.

We were delighted now that we had brought a substantial package of food with us for we intended to go on until we had completed the traverse and face the long tramp back to Coruisk in the moonlight. What a ridge, no difficulty about Sgurr nan Eag, then the delight of Casteal a' Garbh-choire, the roughest piece of gabbro in Skye, vertical rock with large holds. A tin of fruit on Sgurr Dubh na Da Bheinn and we were ready for the Thearlaich-Dubh cap. Doubling the rope, we slid down into it and climbed the rather slippery north wall in a snow shower. It felt quite hard.

On Alastair we met a solitary Israeli who was looking for an easy way down and we showed him the stone Shoot, then did a sharp pitch up Thearlaich, descending the rather holdless slabs which lead to Sgurr Mhic Coinnich. King's Chimney was cold and greasy and the exposed slab at the top was like treading on carefully soaped holds. Then by An Stack to the Inaccessible Pinnacle by its long side. The holds are so good we did not bother to rope up, but uncoiled it on top to swing into space down the far side. The tilt of the rock throws your feet off the wall.

Something was happening to the weather. The peaks which had been playing hide-and-seek with the clouds were now so hard and clear that you could see every detail of buttress, gully and scree. To the west the Outer Hebrides were already blurred by rain and the Torridon hills had disappeared in an approaching murk from the east. The collision of the clouds came on the Bealach na Banachdich as we ate a sandwich. We had been on the tops for six hours, and we reckoned that we needed another five hours to finish the ridge. We were feeling fit and had plenty of food, but there was no point in going on unless we were sure of clear skies and moonlight, otherwise we would only be benighted.

As it happens the rain could not have come at a better place, for the gully leading into the Coruisk basin was well patched with snow and gave us some splendid glissading for most of 1,000 ft, while the rain got heavier and heavier. It was the old familiar downpour by the time we reached the tent and hot soup at 9.15.

It was still raining in the morning, and an amazing thing about the wet tumps we were camped upon was that they did not become any wetter. They were truly afloat, and you could feel them heaving if anyone passed close by. We left the misty Cuillin at 2.30 and were back in our own homes by 10.30 p.m., feeling we had crammed a mighty lot into one weekend. The shared transport costs including the hire of the boat worked out at £1.50 each.

Around the Cuillin is the wettest bit of Skye. The favoured bit of the *Costa* Skye is around Portree, with Raasay within easy reach by car-ferry from Sconser, and roads radiating to the other 'wings' of Skye, to Dunvegan and Duntuilm. There are plenty of things to do, boat trips, bus tours, watching the seals or the birds, or just learning about a way of life where Gaelic is still an everyday language.

I recommend the narrow roads that go out to Glendale and the Boreraig cairn, erected to the memory of the famous MacCrimmon pipers. And if you are at all fit, a visit to the Old Man of Storr is obligatory. You can see it like a leaning chimney-stack just north of Portree. A marked path leads from a high point in the road above the lochs.

Here is quite the opposite of the gabbro geology of Loch Coruisk, which is noble but sterile. The Storr is kindlier. Its pinnacles rise from garden-like turf, cropped by sheep and rabbits. The rock is basalt, loose and friable, but the base rich in minerals on which alpine plants, a profusion of roseroot, globe flowers, yellow mountain saxifrage, alpine ladies' mantle and many another thrives. You have to search much higher up to locate *Koenigia islandica* which grows only here in Britain.

To climb the 2,360-ft flat summit of The Storr it is best to traverse a bit north of The Old Man to clear the rocks, then go straight up over easy ground. From the edge of the plateau there are sensational views down the sheer gullies to the head of the weirdly-balanced Old Man and his decrepit neighbours. It is a good stance too for appreciating the fantastic mixture of scenery which is Skye, ringed by headlands and edged by plunging escarpments of rock, the Outer Hebrides to the west and the ranged summits from Wester Ross to Sutherland to the east.

North, past the scattered crofting township of Staffin, lies the Quirang, only an hour from the road and one of the most dramatic changes of scene in Skye, as you enter a hanging valley, a place of weird knolls and imprisoned pools; surprising, but nothing to the canyon which suddenly opens ahead, with a wall of grey rock on one side and black pinnacles hemming you on the other.

The walking is surprisingly easy to this point on short turf riddled with rabbit holes. But as you get to the pinnacles you start climbing on screes again, not difficult but steep. They twist up to the most unexpected thing of all in this bristling place, the feature marked on the map as 'The Table'. And it is a table, of flat turf, the size of two bowling greens and just as smooth. You would think it was man-made, but it belongs to nature, and the black-faced sheep grazing here are the lawn-mowers.

Standing here is like being on an Everest of a rock garden for the whole cliff above is a hanging garden of flowers in early summer, with sprays of yellow globe flowers, golden roseroot, pendent clumps of mossy and starry saxifrages, huge bunches of red-and-white bladder campion, blue butterwort flowers in every cranny, and even the water avens flowering.

The weird rocks jutting crazily above have names like 'The Prison' and 'The Needle'. By working south along the edge of the table you can drop down an easy gully right below this pinnacle. A sheep path leads to a point where you can walk to the top of the grassy plateau at 1,779 ft. From the north point of Skye to the big hills of Harris seems no distance from here. Look south-east to the green Isle of Raasay and visit it if you can.

Raasay is served by a service ship from Kyle and Portree, but in 1974 a car ferry should operate from Sconser, at the mouth of Loch Sligachan in Skye. It is an island easily overlooked because its thin 14 miles length is overshadowed by the Cuillin, in a sea area that seems to be all fjords and rocky islets backed by wild hills. I had never thought of landing on it myself until I flew over it in a tiny four-seater plane and was immediately drawn to its greenness and the welcoming appearance of a bay that seemed to be crowded with houses. Its woodlands, crofting fields, volcanic plateau and precipitous east coast, destitute of habitation, made me feel I must go back.

I soon discovered that all except a handful of Raasay's 154 people live around Churchtown Bay, many of them in an almost urban settlement unusual in the Highlands. That double row of council-style houses is a legacy, like the excellent deep-water pier, of the iron-ore mining times of the first world war. Crofters only moved in at the end of the last war, when they were offered the houses at £30 each. Since 1931 the population has dropped from 354 to the present low level, due to the scarcity of jobs. The islanders now pin their faith on tourism, and the better communications which have resulted since the car ferry was introduced. To maintain its tradition of Gaelic culture Raasay must hold its young people. In 1972 43 per cent of the population was over 60, but there were 16 children in the primary school, six attending secondary school in Skye, and ten not yet of school age. See what you make of the population level when you go there.

It is a good idea to bring a bicycle to Raasay to have mobility and enjoy the marvellous variety of this geologically exciting island. Cycling along the north coast you almost feel yourself in Skye, except that the view has a panoramic breadth not found on the 'winged isle' itself. From here the crofts of Braes seem to nestle under Sgurr nan Gillean, with the big rock buttress of the Storr towering above a foreground of Raasay's hay fields.

James Gillies of Ballachuirn told me about the crofting situation as he showed me his ten acres of arable land in the bottom of a remote little glen. It had the appearance of a little oasis of fertility because the formation is oolite. The sedimentary rocks are Jurassic. He told me it gave him a fair living. 'I have four cows, but we work our sheep on a club system here, with 2,000 of stock divided into ten shares. It's a good life if you have an interest in the land.'

The fertile oolite soil gives way to Torridonian sandstone just north of Ballachuirn with a dramatic change of scenery cutting right across the island. The deep-cut streams running west are jungles of heather and birches, but the upper Glam Burn is in the oolite zone and gives deep loam between 600 and 900 ft. Sir Frank Fraser Darling regards this depth of loam at such a height as 'Almost unique in the Highlands.' It has been suggested by Heslop-Harrison that parts of Raasay may have escaped the scouring effects of glaciation, judged by this depth of soil and the preservation of a rich flora on the east coast. This is an interesting theory, when you consider that the sea just east of Raasay in the Inner Sound is deeper than anywhere else round the coast of Britain at over 1,000 ft and is believed to be the result of glacial erosion of the softer rocks on the line of the Raasay Fault.

The next dramatic change of scene on Raasay is when the Torridonian sandstone gives way to Archaean gneiss where the road swoops down to the sea at Brochel Castle, perched like a natural pinnacle on its rock. Tottering now, it was nearly intact at the time when Johnson and Boswell visited it in 1773. Dating from the fifteenth–sixteenth century, its three stories must have been a dizzy place to live in.

Beyond Brochel the scenery is reminiscent of the Sutherland coast with pink bones of rock outcropping from the lumpy landscape and steep gullies filled with birches as at Inverkirkaig. The path to Kyle Fladda past the disused school and church is one of the most delightful walks in the Hebrides. Given low tide you can cross to deserted Fladday—there are no crofters left there now. But a Fladday man who left its green pancake for Raasay told me of the time when its little school could muster 60 scholars. The few good houses are used only as holiday homes now.

At the time when Dr Johnson and Boswell were being entertained so royally by MacLeod of Raasay, the island population, including Fladday, was said to be 900. The same figure is quoted for the 1846 period when the last MacLeod sold the island to Mr George Rainy, whose eviction of 94 families within the next three years is still remembered. Thereafter the story follows the classic pattern of conversion to sheep run, then to deer forest. The main owner today is the Department of Agriculture for Scotland, which acquired it in 1922.

Raasay House, alas, has fallen on bad times. Let for shooting until 1937, it operated as a hotel until 1962 when its tenant died. Then it was sold, and work was started on renovations, only to be abandoned. That fine house where Dr Johnson and Boswell slept is falling to bits by neglect. Standing in splendid grounds with one of the finest views in the Highlands before it, the house should be transformed again into the licensed hotel that the island badly needs.

I was thinking of Boswell when I took the track that leads up the edge of the forest to the flat top of Dun Caan where the biographer of Johnson danced a jig of delight. But first I stopped to look at the iron-ore mine perched 400 ft up. The building is only a shell now, but you can see where the aerial ropeway carried the bogeys down to the pier, the actual work of mining being done by 200 German prisoners of the First World War.

Mining was discontinued at the end of hostilities because of the peace-time costs of extraction relative to the low grade of the oolite ironstone. Fresh mineral explorations are going on as I write this and Raasay may yet yield up some treasure. There is oil shale as well as iron ore on Dun Caan. Dun Caan is a neat lava table-top above a plateau cradling blue lochs, a place of cackling red-throated divers and plaintive golden plover.

The view from 1,456 ft stands comparison with any mountain-top panorama in Scotland, encompassing the best of all the Western Highlands, from Kintail to Sutherland and from the Cuillin to the Outer Hebrides.

It is to Kyle of Lochalsh we go now, to explore the land of Kintail and the Applecross peninsula across the Inner Sound from Raasay.

CHAPTER EIGHT

Applecross, Kyle and Kintail

When Sir Frank Fraser Darling published his monumental *West Highland Survey* in 1955, and modestly subtitled it *An Essay in Human Ecology* he singled out the Inner Sound parishes of Applecross, Lochcarron, Lochalsh, Kintail, Glenshiel and Glenelg, as containing some of the remotest townships on this sheltered coast, and saying further that 'it was difficult to point to any good stretch of road.' As for the townships, he pointed out that 'Many have no road at all.'

There has been progress since he wrote these gloomy words. From Kintail by Loch Duich and Glen Shiel to Invergarry on the Great Glen is now a fast motor run on double-width road all the way. North from Kyle you can drive to the head of Loch Carron without the old tedium of queuing to cross by Strome ferry. Shieldaig has been linked to Torridon by the building of six miles of highly scenic road, where previously it meant a 65-mile detour. And now a coast road is being driven all the way round the Applecross peninsula to serve what were formerly the remotest crofting communities in Wester Ross.

The biggest changes, since Darling wrote his book, have been the influence of tourism on the local economy and the boom in property values, caused by the demand for homes, for holiday, or permanent occupation by southerners wishing to opt out of the rat race. Crofting, allied to an income from 'Bed and Breakfast', is being seen as a good way of life.

Nor is remoteness regarded as awkward in these radio-and-television times if you can get your motor car to the front door. Take Applecross, for example, reached from Loch Kishorn in a 2,000-ft climb, zigzagging, alpine fashion, into a wild corrie, then plunging again down to sea level on a shore of limestone greensward with a delightful row of white cottages making a village street facing out to Skye. Everything about the place is attractive, including the coast road southward, which winds through the crofting township to end at Toscaig pier.

The place has a Hebridean feel, emphasized if you choose to arrive by sea on the morning or afternoon boat from Kyle of Lochalsh. It is a popular excursion with tourists and lasts just under three hours. On my last visit by this boat we landed with our bicycles and lightweight camping kit to explore the wild north coast which has not yet been opened to motor cars.

Easy cycling ends in four miles at Applecross village, where the public road turns from the shore to climb over the Bealach nam Bo. Our way lay straight ahead, by the motor-cycle track climbing at a remorseless gradient to turn the seaward shoulder of the hill in front. By the time we got to the top we were ready to camp, on a shelf facing out to the whole rampart of the Harris hills, while far below were two fishing boats, mere toys on the wrinkled sea, emphasizing the scale of this fretted coast.

An anger of red flaring clouds at sunset gave us the feeling that nature was making some sort of pronouncement. By morning the message had been delivered with wind and rain as we followed the contouring path in a diminished world of drizzle and enveloping cloud. Then down we plunged, to a neat little bay called Sand, to rise again between the walls of a close-sided glen of cliffs and birches. It led to the first crofting settlement, Lonbain.

I wondered about the crofts on the headland. The numerous strips of green made a big quilt but were reverting to rough pasture, yet I knew this land to be equal to the best on Raasay just across the water, for it is of the same oolite formation, and it grew good crops not so long ago. There was no sign of life round the derelict houses, only sheep.

The next crofting township told the same story, then, just as I was thinking we had stepped into a completely lifeless world, there was a reassuring sight. Over a knoll suddenly appeared a postman, mounted on his red bicycle. John Gordon was the very man to tell us the things we wanted to know. He was on his way to deliver mail to the only men who still live in Lonbain, both of them bachelors. After that he would return to his own village of Cuaig—population three families.

25 *Crofting at Churchton Bay above the Narrows of Raasay, Skye across the water*

26 *Raasay crofters shearing sheep*

John Gordon told me he had been on the beat for 25 years, covering 19 miles every day, about half of which has to be walked. All this to serve 13 houses, including his own. He has seen the gradual passing of crofting as people died off or gave up. At the township of Kalnakill where we talked, the last man had just moved out. When he found he was the only one left he decided to move to Applecross, but his sheep are still at Kalnakill.

John then went on to talk about the new road winding round the coast from Shieldaig to Kenmore and now pushing over from Loch Torridon to reach Applecross somewhere around 1975. 'It will make this place busy, for I'm told that the Estate Office has had over 250 applications for the empty houses you passed today. But I'm wondering if there will be any need for me when a motor van goes on the mail run'. Another titbit of information was the marking of the coast of Raasay, Rona and Applecross, for the testing of torpedoes when a proposed Admiralty naval base comes to Kyle. These waters of the Inner Sound where the torpedoes will be tested are deeper than any other coastal region of Britain, with bottom at over 1,000 ft.

John's village of Cuaig lay just a couple of miles ahead of us, perched above a bay, with Loch Torridon out of sight round the corner. Three families, but with three children out of a total population of ten, this could be said to be the liveliest township between Kenmore and Applecross. One of the men is a herring fisherman with a local boat, the other is a crofter. Nearest neighbours are at Fearnmore and Fearnbeg, just two miles north by a path, where half-a-dozen elderly people live.

Round the corner on that Torridon shore I met a spry old man, who, like me, was a visitor. But it was only when we had talked for a little while I discovered that he was an Applecross man, who had gone to school here. 'Look at these God-built harbours,' he expostulated. 'Every one of them was full of boats when I was a boy. In Arrinas where I went to school there were forty scholars. We even had our own tailor and shoemaker in these days, and the people grew flax to make their own shirts.'

He painted a vivid word picture of his boyhood before the decline. 'Life was different in those days, because there was always a coming-and-going of boats. Schooners used to call to buy the fish, and later on the men took it to Shieldaig for sending to the railway. People

27   *Raasay, the view from Dun Caan 1,456 ft, looking to the peaks of Skye*

28   *Loch Coruisk in Skye, the most exciting rock basin in Scotland*

lived mainly on what they could grow or catch, and if they needed anything they could buy it from travelling boats rigged out as shops. You didn't miss a road in these days.'

I asked him why he had left Applecross. He pondered the question and put his finger on the answer this way:

'Well, the fish got scarce. When I was young it was common to catch a hundred crans of herring in a day, and there was any amount of white fish for the catching. We lived on fish and potatoes and meal. It was the same out on the island of Lewis, but they suffered even more than we did by foreign trawlers working too close to the shore. You had to leave to seek your fortune. I went to Glasgow and became a shoemaker. If we had had a road into the townships of North Applecross it might have been different.'

My own view is that a road by itself could not have made a great deal of difference, unless it was backed by a fighting plan to protect the fisheries, help the crofters to build bigger boats, and lay out warehouses and fish factories as the Norwegians and the Faroese have done. But Applecross men were neither induced by grants nor subsidies to stay.

And there was certainly no adequate living to be had from crofting without fishing, when the whole of the peninsula was sporting estate with the best land in the hands of two owners. The crunch came, however, in 1964 when the remaining crofters demanded a road, and one of the landowners played into their hands by saying he did not want the region to be opened up, that the crofters of Applecross were happy as they were.

He was instantly challenged by Alexander MacKenzie of Arrinas, who demanded to know the names and addresses of the 'happy crofters'. And he added: 'The history of the Highlands can amply verify what we have suffered in the past because of absentee landlords. Surely the County Council of Ross and Cromarty should not be dictated to by Mr Greig in the middle of the twentieth century.'

These fighting words alerted Press and Television, especially when a published statement by the Development Officer for the County recommended the evacuation of the 55 crofters of North Applecross in preference to the expensive undertaking of a road. The Ross and Cromarty Planning Committee decided in favour of the crofters by publishing a further statement which read:

Access to the area is by boat, or by a narrow footpath. After considering the report, the planning committee of the County Council appointed a sub-committee to investigate the possibility of forming a road less expensive than the normal county highway but capable of permitting vehicular access to some of the scattered communities along the coast, as preferable to some of the proposals mentioned in the county development officer's report.

But the County Development Officer had done a good job, by bringing into the open the shameful neglect of one of the most beautiful corners of the Highlands. For if public services had been withdrawn or a 'minimum access' scheme approved, then the sporting landlord would indeed have had it all his own way.

The finished road which now stretches along the line of the old 'wall of death' motor-cycle track has brought vitality in its wake. New crofters have moved in, one of them a Yorkshireman. Children are collected every day and taken to school in Shieldaig. Visitors enliven the place and pay for 'Bed and Breakfast'. The exchange is good for everyone. The contrast is striking between those who have the road and those who do not.

Applecross just over a hundred years ago had nearly 3,000 inhabitants, and living standards must have been poor, with crofts sub-divided to a point of acute land hunger. It was natural that the greater opportunities opening up elsewhere in Scotland should cause a drift from the Highlands. But the failure to arrest the slide by tackling the real cause of the disaster was baulked. The easy way was to let the people go, and obtain rateable valuations from the sporting revenue of the estate. Indeed one-fifth of the rateable valuations of Ross and Cromarty were obtained from shootings and deer forests as recently as in 1914. It has been the road to ruin for the indigenous people of the Highlands.

Here is a fragment of conversation I wrote down nearly 20 years ago with the MacRaes of Camusterrach, who happened to see me pass and invited me in for tea. 'Yes, a lovely place Applecross,' said the man as I was handed home-baked scones and pancakes still warm from the girdle, 'if you could live on scenery, but you can't. That is why there are only old folk and young children in the parish. How many able-bodied men have you seen in Applecross since you came?' I had to admit I had seen only one or two.

'Yes, just a few. And you know what will happen to their children? The same as happened to mine; they will leave Applecross to get their secondary schooling and they won't come back. That will be the end of them except as summer visitors, for there is nothing for them here.'

'What about the fishing?' I asked, knowing that South Applecross was primarily a fishing parish, using the Inner Sound coastal waters. 'That was in the past,' he replied. 'Of fourteen boats that used to fish herring and white fish there is only one left. That is why in any township in Applecross you will find a dozen old-age pensioners for each able-bodied man. Take this place, for example. None of the people who lived here when I came to this township are living here now. And no young ones are following on, because the only way to get a living here is to have plenty of sheep and cattle, but you need land for that, and we have not got it.'

Well that was Mr MacRae, a man with a family of eight who had put one son through university and was doing the same for another at that moment. As a subsistence crofter with a public road to his door he described himself as well off compared to the people of the Loch Torridon shore who had only the 'wall of death' track giving them access to the outside world.

Things are better today in Mr MacRae's country. Three local boats are fishing for prawns, and a young man in his prime told me there are 15 of his own age group in the place, and that none of them wanted to leave. The primary school roll was 20 on that 1971 visit.

I think the growing enthusiasm of holidaymakers to the Highlands and Islands is having a rub-off effect on the young, who are constantly hearing about the disenchantment of overcrowded life in the cities where more and more money is needed to buy less and less. Yet it is unlikely that the brightest young scholars of the West Highlands will stay in their villages, for they tend to be ambitious and clever. The professions draw them like steel to a magnet. They have to prove themselves, make good, and usually do, but their vigour is lost to the Highlands.

Meantime in 1972, at the time of writing, the Gaelic-speaking population of Applecross totals 60 per cent of the whole, supporting the truth that relative isolation is a major factor in keeping alive the old language and customs. The future is going to be interesting as all Applecross is opened up by coast road, and with it a heavy dilution of English-speaking incomers will inevitably follow.

One strange story I got from an old crofter in Applecross is worth retelling. It concerns Mr Hare, of Burke and Hare, the body-snatchers.

'Did you know that Hare was an Applecross man by adoption?' my informant quizzed. Then he told me of how, after Hare had turned King's Evidence, he settled in Applecross, where nobody asked any questions, did well as a weaver, got married and died a respected citizen.

A curious story. I know that Hare is commonly supposed to have ended his days as a blind beggar in London, but is this fact or conjecture? He was an Irish labourer, and it is not easy to accept him as a skilled weaver. But the old man said that the story had long been current in Applecross and said he himself believed it.

There is no doubt at all about St Maelrubha, the red-haired Irish saint of royal birth who missionized here in the manner of St Columba, and was similarly revered. The site of his mission was by the river, from where he carried the faith for about 50 years until his death in 722, when his body was brought back from Sutherland to be buried here.

Searching for his grave in the long grass of the churchyard, I found what I was looking for near the ruins of the old chapel, two rounded stubs of boulders, a body-width apart. Tradition says that this is the grave of the saint, who established a wide sanctuary round the river, inside whose stones any refugee was safe. If the Burke and Hare story is true, then history repeated itself in the most strange of ways. The right of sanctuary in Applecross ended with the Reformation.

Now let's think of the drive from Applecross Bay east by the Bealach nam Bo, turning your back on Raasay and Skye for the big climb from the fertile lias to the bare Torridonian sandstone of the pass in all its strangeness of pink rocks and trapped lochans. Then the plunge down from the summit at 2,000 ft into a more vertical world, where the road is a mere ledge on the thrusting face. Indeed hard rock climbs can be begun 200 ft above your car, while just across the narrow corrie is the wall of Meall Gorm, its soaring *arête* framing the view of Loch Kishorn and the high peaks of Glen Affric.

No other road in the west climbs so high and so quickly, and in an icy winter it can be a formidable problem. Contouring round the nose of Sgurr à Chaorachain and over the Russel Burn it eases down gently to the road junction at Tornapress, where the north fork goes to Shieldaig, and the south to Kyle. On a fine day it is worth going north for a mile, even if your route is south, to enjoy the contrast of Rassal ash wood, where limestone changes the moorland from Torridonian brown to bright emerald, and scattered on the steepening slope are the silvery trunks of gnarled trees.

May is the time to see this green place, when the wood rings with bird song, yet just across the glen the rock corries of Ben Bhan still carry winter snow. The rock climber will find plenty of scope for new routes over there, yet down here you walk on a carpet of thick moss spattered with flowers and sapling ash trees. By fencing 30 acres against sheep, the Nature Conservancy has given this fragment of natural woodland a chance to reproduce itself. Even the pied fly-catcher has bred here in recent times.

Turning south you are very soon back in green country again, for Loch Kishorn bears a strip of Dolomitic limestone a full five miles by one mile, and it should be lingered over by exploring down to the south corner of the bay, which lies two miles off the public road.

Look across to the Bealach nam Bo from here and notice the double-barrel of rock known as the Cioch on Sgurr à Chaorachain, whose 600-ft vertical nose was climbed by Chris Bonington and Tom Patey in 1958, proving itself to be very much easier than it looked, but sensationally steep. For me it has sad associations, for I climbed it with the late Tom Patey just a few days before that most remarkable of Scottish mountaineers was killed in May 1970.

East from Loch Kishorn on the road to Kyle, a wild little ravine leads you back to the sea on Loch Carron and a long village street of neatly kept houses. The story here is of Applecross all over again, a population of over 2,000 living by fishing and being forced to move when it failed in the mid-nineteenth century. In the philosophy of these times the natives could always emigrate, help support the great British Empire, and leave land unencumbered by their presence to the new rich who bought it up for its grouse, its salmon fishing and deer stalking.

It used to be that you had to keep to the north side of Loch Carron and cross by Strome Ferry to regain the road to Kyle. Now you must take the south side and join the new road built alongside the railway. This sub-standard road has a bad record. Opened in 1969 it was blocked three times by avalanches in its first two years, perhaps fortunately, for it made a good case for the retention of the railway in the face of threatened closure in 1972. It has been reprieved until 1974, but the future of this superbly scenic line is uncertain as I write this.

The new road, single width with numerous passing places, is attractive, dominated by tall spruces on the east and giving fine glimpses of Skye ahead and the villages of Loch Carron across the loch. Round a spur and you come to Strome ferry, the former terminus of the Dingwall and Skye Railway from 1870 until 1897. Here for the first time in history the people of the West Highlands could connect by rail and ship from Atlantic to North Sea. The railway company ran the ships to Skye and Stornoway in connection with the trains.

To push the line the last 10½ miles along the rocky coast to Lochalsh cost £20,000 per mile and four years of blasting and bridging, the most expensive piece of railway engineering to that date. But in recognition of the social need of the service, the Government gave £45,000, to help the fish trade and for the carriage of mails.

Over the forested hill by a dog-leg and you face a wider Loch Carron, or strike away from it, due south to Loch Alsh. I recommend the former route to Kyle, which threads under the Duncraig Castle crags for a view of Plockton in the most picturesque setting of any village in the West Highlands.

Plockton used to live by fishing. Mrs Jean McKenzie who travelled on the very first passenger train into Kyle, on 2 November 1897, told me about these times, when everybody spoke Gaelic, and people had to carry water and cut peats if they would have a fire in winter. 'Plockton was a more private place then. You could call your own doorstep your own. Now with so many cars and campers it's like Dingwall.' She also remembered that the village had five shops when she was a girl. Now it has one, and half the houses are holiday homes owned by absentees from England.

But Plockton has a new high school and dormitories for boarding pupils from outlying corners of south-west Ross, and was the first base of the top-gallant-yard schooner *Captain Scott* used in Outward-Bound training courses. Local yachtsmen hold regattas there in summer and they are often joined by weekenders from the stockbroker belt of London, who fly to Glasgow and take a charter flight by Loganair to land on the tiny airstrip behind the village.

South again, by the croft of Durinish and Drumbuie, you join the main road and arrive in Kyle, the metropolis of these parts, population 600, with a shuttle service of ferries to Skye, and usually traffic congestion in summer near the ferry slip. Kyle was just a croft house or two until the railway blasted its way through and the terminus took on the grandiose name of Kyle of Lochalsh. And because it is of such recent origin it is a cosmopolitan place, easy for a newcomer to fit into.

'We were in Portree for a couple of years,' said a young couple I spoke to, 'but we always felt outsiders. Kyle is a much more friendly place.' I heard other new residents enthusing in similar fashion. One of them said, 'I'm keen on golf. We have a local club. The wee course out at the Ploc must have the finest view of any course in Scotland, and visitors really enjoy it. The maintenance of it is typical of this place. When jobs have to be done we all muck in and do them. I take along my rotary scythe, somebody else brings a lawnmower, a scythe or a few tools and there it is.'

There is also a local fieldclub, which is so popular that 80 or 90 members turn out for meetings, which because of the scattered membership, are held in different places—Kyle, Plockton, Dornie or wherever is convenient. The bank manager, from Speyside, told me that the social life is so rich that you will be busy if you manage to keep up with it. Naturally it was from Kyle that the main opposition to the closure of the railway came.

Councillor Torquil Nicolson, who led the objectors, used to be Manager for the North of Scotland Hydro-Electric Board. He told me: 'I came to Kyle, at a smaller salary, and when I retired in 1965 I thought I would have plenty of time for sailing and doing a bit of landscape painting . . . that's still a dream. When you live in the Highlands you soon find out that you have to run like mad to keep from going backwards. You can't sit back and do nothing about it. I don't regard it as a sacrifice if things get done that might not have been done.'

To appreciate the strategic position of Kyle it is necessary to get some height, and if the day be clear there is nowhere better than the small hill above the railway station. From up there you can appreciate that this is a turning point of waterways with a freeway north up the straight Applecross coast, or eastward into the more sheltered waters of Loch Alsh giving access to the Sound of Sleat, or into Kintail by the big arm of Loch Duich.

The Skye coast looks very close, with the thirteenth-century ruin of Casteil Maoil just across the water dating to the Norse period, when the Vikings controlled this strait and forced passing ships to pay tribute. Kyleakin, beside the castle, takes its name from King Hakon, and the nearest of the high Cuillin, the double peak of Blaven, is the Norse for blue mountain—well named.

Back to your car and speeding east, you are on something very rare in the Western Highlands, a fast, modern, double-width road running along the shore of Loch Alsh and continuing all the way by Loch Duich and Glen Shiel through some of the most varied scenery within the scope of this book. The temptation to speed on should be resisted or you will be the loser.

A good first place to stop is the National Trust for Scotland information centre at Reraig on the east side of Balmacara Bay, where tree-trunk tables and sawn-log chairs invite a picnic. The Trust have laid out a few attractive spots like this, to invite visitors to stop, have a snack and enjoy the view. Balmacara House itself is leased to the education authority for training boys in agriculture, horticulture and carpentry.

The meeting place of the three sea lochs is Ardelve and Dornie, with crofting fields and dotted white houses on opposite shores of narrow Loch Long, and beneath them, at the junction of Loch Duich with Loch Alsh, the most photographed castle in Scotland, Eilean Donan, quickly accessible by bridge between mainland and island.

Picture-postcard and chocolate-box familiarity may blunt the imagination, but the reality of Eilean Donan does not disappoint, when the eye ranges on it against the wide horizon of Kintail peaks, with the near charm of woods, green knolls and human settlement above the changing surface of the waters.

The present solid structure is a 1932 reconstruction of a thirteenth-century castle erected against the Vikings then in Skye, and destroyed by British frigates in the forgotten Jacobite adventure of 1719 whose aftermath was the battle of Glen Shiel, commemorated to this day in the peak of Sgurr na Spainteach, named after Spaniards who surrendered to the Government forces.

Until that bombardment, the MacRaes were keepers of Eilean Donan, in alliance with the Mackenzies, who had held it from the sixteenth century. Appropriately in this MacRae country, it was a wealthy descendant of the clan who rebuilt it, Lt.-Col. John MacRae-Gilstrap, in 20 years of endeavour costing £¼ million. The replica is said to be a true restoration of the original and there is plenty of interest, domestic and defensive, inside to make a visit worthwhile.

The Fall of Glomach is a must for anyone excited by wild gorges and thundering waterfalls. There is no absolutely easy way to it, but if you don't mind driving on a rough road and climbing for an hour on a narrow footpath, then you should take the road out of Ardelve across Dornie Bridge. At Killilan you have to sign the visitors' book to proceed on the private road to the point where the Glomach stream comes out of its cavern to the south. The parking place is obvious and the footpath is marked. You will need two hours for the return journey.

The gorge is a box canyon which becomes steeper-sided as you go up the threading path. You hear the fall before you see it, and the best place for a view is a rocky platform half way down the gorge and reached by a zigzagging slippery path demanding care. Opposite you now the water curls over a headwall as a white ribbon, is split into two by a black pinnacle, hurtling on as separate columns then joining-up to plunge as a solid force again for a final throw into neck-craning gloom. In this natural sound box of a canyon the roar and the movement of the hurtling water makes the mind spin. The plunge in total is over 350 ft, but it seems a lot more, and most people are glad to climb out.

A good round trip is to come out from the Fall and cross the hills to the head of Loch Duich by the narrow pass of the Bealach na Sroine leading down to Dorusduain Lodge and Strath Croe in about three hours. This implies having a companion to pick you up. If it has to be a one-way trip I recommend the shorter Loch Long approach by Glen Elchaig as the most rewarding in interest.

Other fine routes from Morvich on Loch Duich lead right across from the Atlantic to North Sea, north to Loch Monar and Glen Strathfarrar, or into Glen Affric by Glen Lichd via Altbeath youth hostel. These are wild walks. One I did was from Glen Cannich, climbing 2,300 ft by Gleann a' Choilich in a May snow-storm and plunging down to Glen Affric in the rain.

Glen Lichd was the home stretch, walled by Ben Fhada on one side, with the Kintail Sisters on the other, mountain torrents foaming down from each green slope, and only glimpses of the whitened tops showing through the swirling mist. Then out came the sun as I dropped to the seashore, where eider ducks and red-throated divers were disporting themselves. It felt so mild down there that it was hard to believe that it was still winter on the glittering tops.

In summer time there is nothing difficult about the hills of Kintail. Frankly I find them monotonously green and lacking in climbing interest, but they have the wonderful feature of being linked together by high ridges and once you have done the hard work of grinding your way to the first top you can stride out and take in peak after peak.

They really look better from the glens, especially if you motor down Glen Shiel from the bleakness of Loch Cluanie as the road begins to drop and the spearpoint of Faochag and the cleft peak of The Saddle dominate. The Five Sisters opposite them are not seen to advantage here and are best appreciated by taking the left fork at the foot of the glen for the twisting steep climb up the Mam Ratagan.

Good lay-bys beyond the conifers enable you to see out to Glen Shiel and the range of the Sisters dominating Loch Duich. The plunge down the other side to Glenelg is hardly less exciting, and down there of course we link to our earlier explorations in Knoydart and Skye. Bernera barracks in three-storied ruin dates back to the times immediately following the blowing up of Eilean Donan Castle, when the Government built them for a force of troops which occupied them until near the close of the nineteenth century.

Infinitely older and more interesting ruins can be seen in nearby Glen Beag, a charming green place of farms and woods which may lose its character if over-planted by the Forestry Commission. Just two miles up you see the first of the brochs, Dun Telve, an Iron-age tower of great double walls, mostly collapsed, but standing 30 ft high on one side. Dun Troddan, its neighbour, lies only a short distance ahead.

The brochs are something of a mystery, like the Picts who built them for defence, and they are found only in Scotland. Like Eilean Donan, they were built against the Vikings most probably, in the times when the Norsemen were sporadic raiders rather than an occupying force.

Now we shall return to Kyle and go north to Glen Carron and over the hills to Torridon. But pause as you cross the causeway, at the head of Loch Duich, which cuts off the loop at Morvich and was the last part of the Invergarry to Kyle of Lochalsh road, completed in 1972 after a decade of building.

Look at the seaward side of this half mile of causeway, composed of great blocks of stone, each one weighing over half a ton, and placed individually on the 2:1 slope after being quarried in Glen Shiel. The road had to be supported this way because the local granite fragmented too easily.

CHAPTER NINE

The Torridonian Landscape

Torridon, Loch Maree, Gairloch and Poolewe—
Fisherfield—Loch Broom—Ullapool—Coigach

In the last chapter we had our first glimpse of the Torridonian
landscape in the rampart of the Bealach nam Bo. This striking formation reappears in Glen Carron at Achnashellach, in the thrusting
crags of Fuar Toll and its neighbours of the Coulin Forest. Over these
hills and exactly parallel with Glen Carron lies Glen Torridon, whose
greatest extravagance is the peak of Liathach, built layer on layer of
sandstone and rising to a dramatically peaky top.

Motorists have to continue to Achnasheen and swing west over the
pass to Kinlochewe to enter Glen Torridon. Hill walkers have some
thrilling alternatives from Achnashellach, by the Coulin Pass and
Loch Clair in eight comfortable miles for the most thrilling first views
of the glen possible. Or by footpaths climbing high into wild corries
and dropping down to Annat at the head of Loch Torridon.

It was by the Coulin Pass I first came to Glen Torridon, humping a
huge rucksack from Achnashellach, toiling up, descending the River
Coulin, turning a corner and there was Liathach, an enormous
black hump in the moonlight, sheer-sided like a haystack and only
slightly squatter in shape.

I had read about the ancient rocks of Torridon, and the remnants of
primeval pine forest growing on moraines where pine martens and
wild cats still roamed. The reality was even better than expectation
when morning came and from our camp we looked beyond the
frosted grass to the sparkle of quartzite peaks glittering like snow above
Loch Clair. What a contrast between the ridges of Ben Eighe covered
with quartzite screes almost to the bottom, and the brown-pink

barrel hoops of Liathach banding the peak in terrace after terrace of Torridonian sandstone.

Impossible not to feel romance. The pines had been growing here for something like 8,000 years. The floor of the glen, grey and ice-scored, was the very floor of the world—Lewisean gneiss over 2,000 million years old. Even the sandstone, rising layer upon layer to over 3,000 ft had been laid down before there was any life on earth, dating back over 1,000 million years. Only the younger quartzite contains fossils, worm casts of the earliest life.

In crisp clear weather we traversed the ridge of Ben Eighe, looked down on the triple buttress of Coire Mhic Fhearchair and resolved that one day we would come back and make routes up their 1,300-ft verticalities. Liathach fulfilled our high expectations, with pinnacles and wild north-facing corries through which we scrambled. From Ben Alligin we looked beyond the Cuillin of Skye to the Outer Hebrides—my first Atlantic prospect. On Sgurr Ruadh we frightened ourselves on difficult and exposed rocks. From Slioch we saw a promised land of mountains impossible to explore except by hard pack-carrying into the interior of roadless country lying between Little Loch Broom and Loch Maree.

Over the years I fulfilled my climbing dreams in many spring, autumn and winter visits, but the excitement which Glen Torridon induced in me on that first teen-age visit is undiminished. My favourite way of arriving is to leave my rucksack at Achnasheen to be sent round by mail bus to Annat, while I go on to Achnashellach to strike up into Coire Lair on a superb footpath curling round between the peaks of Fuar Toll and Ben Liath Mhor. On the col below Sgor Ruadh you are half way to Loch Torridon, and a wonderful descent lies ahead, first a traverse through a complicated little world of peaklets, then over the neck of Bealach na Lice among rock slabs and lochans in a litter of glacial rubble. The path down leads exactly to Annat village.

One day at the end of February I had a struggle with my conscience as to which route I should take at Achnashellach. I had intended to do the walk described above, but the peak of Fuar Toll shining in icy splendour against a blue sky tempted me to a more ambitious under-taking. A small voice was telling me that I might live a lifetime and never see the mountain in such perfect condition again. 'Think of the view,' it said, 'and you could keep to the crest of the ridge all the way over Sgurr Ruadh and drop directly to the Bealach na Lice. You could be in Annat in two hours from there.'

I gripped my ice-axe tighter, slung my rucksack and left caution behind me among the green pines whose snow tinsel was not even dripping in the sunlight. Eager to get off the deep snow, I took to the rocks where a sandstone band cuts the upper part from the lower, dividing easy walking from real mountaineering. Nicking steps with my axe in the hardening ice-cover, I was soon on more knobbly rock, enjoying a steep staircase of clean holds.

This is the kind of work I love—Alpine rather than Scottish—not easy but not too hard. I was on the edge of a buttress. An icy gully plunged down on my right. Beyond it was another buttress soaring to a corniced ege, the summit, not far off now.

Absorbed in the final wall of hard snow and green ice I was suddenly douched in a whirling torment of snow spume, so blinding that I had to close my eyes and hold tight against the gusts of wind that jabbed like body blows. Within minutes the gloves holding my ice-axe became stiff with frost. And, by that time, an uncomfortable cold spray was forcing its way down my neck and finding chinks in my anorak. This was no longer fun but survival.

'Surely the weather couldn't get drastic quite as suddenly as this! It must be a short squall,' I was thinking, as I hacked out a staircase, anorak flapping in the wind, eyes watering as I tried to see rock holds. Then a great moment. The slope lay back, and I walked out into relative calm.

The curling lip of any steep mountain is a notably draughty place, and I had been merely getting the full force of the funnel effect as a strong north wind hit the sheltered side up which I had been climbing. Something *had* happened to the weather however. I was in the clouds. It was snowing, and I could feel the wind getting stronger even in the time it took me to take a compass bearing to Sgurr Ruadh.

If the conditions had been white-out, I would have wasted no time in dropping to Coire Lair. I decided to press on because I was still master of the situation. I had been in fiercer wind and snow. I felt strong and reasonably warm in body, so I pushed on as hard as I was able.

So, head down, in a whirl of snowflakes, I picked my way to the col, found the ice-igloo of the cairn on Sgurr Ruadh, continued north-west on snow that was remarkably easy going, then struck hard west down steep invisible slopes. Wonderful moment when out of nothing materialized a dark oval which did not move with the clouds. Loch Coire Fionnaraich.

Mountaineers marooned in storm know the glad feeling when suddenly you find yourself where you hope your steps have been leading you. The heart never fails to leap when you pierce the clouds. And with gladness I sat myself down in the convenient gully plunging away beneath me and slid down in a fast sitting glissade.

Down there I was on the Bealach na Lice path, only two hours away Loch Torridon, but it was an arctic world, absolutely without life until I came to the first trees. Then round a bluff and below me were the friendly lights of Annat gleaming in the dusk, and all I had to do was step inside to dinner with the crofting friends who were expecting me.

At the end of a snowy week I was glad I had taken my chance of the tops for on no other day was it possible to go high, as March came in like a lion, roaring over the peaks with hail and blizzard, through which you would sometimes see long snow plumes smoking from the ridges. It was exciting enough on the low ground, and with a companion I used the mail bus to get dropped off at various places in the glen, so that we could walk back home by a variety of routes. The daily mail bus enables the walker to explore behind the peaks of Glen Torridon. Getting off at the ruins where the Coire Dubh path breaks into the hills, we did the traverse round the north face of Liathach on a day of boiling black clouds and escaping rays of sunshine, enjoying the sudden transformations as the splintered pinnacles broke clear above the whole 3,000-ft wall of the mountain, the whole in steaming turmoil.

That is a walk which should not be missed, leading through the best peaks of Torridon and back to the loch by the Coire Mhic Nobhil pines. The actual distance is about six miles with a rise of no more than 1,000 ft and the path goes all the way, though my Ordnance Survey map does not show it as threading the lochans of the summit.

The mail bus can also be used to advantage for exploring the pines and birches of Loch Clair and Loch Coulin by the Coulin Lodge track, which is a photographic must for the finest aspect of mighty Liathach. Visit it in October when the birches are gold

29 *Picturesque Plockton in Wester Ross. Behind it rise the peaks of Applecross over Loch Carron*

30 *Eilean Donan Castle, looking out on Loch Alsh*

against the loch and the tops have the first brush of winter snow and you will see it at its best. A path from Loch Coulin leads gently over the hill to Kinlochewe.

From Annat itself there is a fine walk just above the hotel, following the burn to an impressive waterfall. Continuing on, you can break east by a little col which brings you out at Loch an Eoin on the Bealach na Lice path and follow it back to Annat. Nor should the old coastal track beneath the new Shieldaig road be neglected.

Annat as a crofting township has declined drastically since I knew it first. I discussed this with one of my Gaelic-speaking friends in 1972. He spelled it out for me. 'There are only five families of original inhabitants left. From 50 people 50 years ago we are down to ten now. When we're gone it will be like Kinlochewe—almost an English village.'

A friend of mine, anxious to leave London and settle in the High-lands, tried to buy a house in Shieldaig further west along the loch. The price asked was £3,500. Given a good survey report, he intended to buy it and make it his home. But the Inverness surveyor who charged him £30 for his inspection, told him it was worth perhaps £2,500, and even at that it would need £1,000 spent on it. But the seller was not prepared to negotiate. The house did in fact sell for £3,750, despite rising damp within and one side of the roof needing re-slating.

My friend found the house he was looking for on the other side of the loch at Inver Alligin, one that smelt sweet and had been cared for, with an unobstructed view to Liathach and the sharp peaks across Loch Torridon, which gives this fjord such Norwegian character. That was in the mid-1960s. Now after eight years he and his wife say they would rather die than go back to London. My friend put it to me this way: 'We feel we have a future that we can believe in. The frustrating sense that we were wasting our lives has gone. You need only to look out of that window for reassurance. We belong to a community that is worth integrating into.'

How do they manage to live? They run their home as a guest house in summer, and manufacture children's toys in winter. And strangely enough their own children have more playmates here than they ever had in London. Inver Alligin lies roughly opposite Shieldaig on the north side of Loch Torridon, and from it a track goes round the shore to Diabaig, looking out to the crofts of North Applecross at Kenmore.

31   *Crofters of Duirinish: communal potato planting*

32   *John Gordon, the postman of Applecross*

33   *A crofter of Duirinish, near Plockton*

But the normal route to Diabaig is by the narrow road over the hill by the Bealach na Goaithe at 750 ft, to make a curving descent through the crofts of this delightful settlement on the north shore of a sheltered horseshoe of bay. Diabaig formerly lived by crofting and fishing, like the Applecross townships across the loch, and a relic of these times remains in persistence to the old way of life, even to some boat building.

There is no outlet from the village north, except by footpath, but no doubt in time a road will be built up the coast to Red Point, which would give a motoring route to Gairloch. Meantime it belongs to the walker, whose slow speed is just right for taking in the mighty prospect of islands and sea, with out there the north tip of Skye, Rona, Lewis and Harris.

The motorist must return to Torridon by the way he has come, and he should take the opportunity of trying out the new Applecross road before leaving Loch Torridon. It strikes off from Loch Shieldaig at the most westerly stand of Caledonian pines in Scotland. Sheltered from the prevailing westerlies these trees are only one of the signs that this side of the loch is a more kindly place to live than the other. The first village is Ardheslaig on a little oasis of a peninsula below the road, a perfect God-built harbour with little sheltering inlets on each side, and even a herring boat with a local crew.

Kenmore lies over the hill in the curve of a bay with a fine outlook. Walkers should note the footpaths crossing directly through the hills to converge on Applecross village. Now we must turn to new territory and speed back to take a closer look at the changing land use of Glen Torridon.

The most striking thing about it now is that it has almost the status of a National Park, with the National Trust for Scotland and the Nature Conservancy jointly owning the whole north side and playing a great part in opening it up by the sign-posting of paths, providing literature at their information offices in Torridon and Kinlochewe, and building nature trails.

Ben Eighe was, in fact, Britain's first National Nature Reserve, acquired in 1951 because of its primeval landscape and fragment of natural pine forest, best seen in Coile na Glas Leitire above Loch Maree, a short distance north of Kinlochewe. Park your car and take a walk up the nature trail and discover more about this landscape with help of a trail pamphlet obtainable from a box at the start of the walk.

The Chief Warden here is Dick Balharry, who was a gamekeeper and deerstalker with the Red Deer Commission before coming to Ben Eighe. He explained his philosophy of the trail to me. 'We hear a lot of talk about conservation, but I see it as useless unless there are people to enjoy it, and marvel at it. In the past in the Highlands there has been too much killing. I've done it myself as a deer stalker. I've killed 22 wildcats in a year, and I've shot deer until I was sick of myself for doing it.'

'But deer have to be shot. We aim to kill a sixth of the total number of stags every year. This is conservation in action. You can't do it without endangering life if you have a lot of climbers wandering about. Nor can you hope to keep people off all the hills during the sporting season. You've got to have an information system which lets the public know when and where deer stalking is in progress. So we display maps on all access paths, and in hotels, showing the location of the nearest house where up-to-the-minute information can be obtained; and if deer stalking happens to be in progress on any given hill, the intending climber will be given a choice of alternative routes in the vicinity. The 50 maps we have on display also show tent sites, hotels, and residential areas.

'The idea of having an information centre, a deer park and a nature trail is to stimulate people into realizing the enormous scope of this region from the head of Loch Torridon to Loch Maree, get them out of their motor cars to really look at the place'.

With the numbered markers on the trail and the explanatory pamphlets, the story gradually unfolds as you climb through the pines to a geological plinth commanding a view of the roadless shore under Slioch. Having had the rock structure explained to you in the pamphlet, and with evidence of the plinth, which is a sandwich composed of Lewisean gneiss below, Torridonian sandstone in the middle, and Cambrian quartzite on top, you see how Slioch, across the Loch, is a pyramid of pink sandstone resting at near mid-height on grey bosses of gneiss, the summit itself having a little cap of the pale quartzite.

You will also learn that there were ironworks on that far shore 350 years ago, consuming 20 acres of oaks daily for the making of charcoal. The way to that shore is by the Heights of Kinlochewe, and I shall not readily forget one March trip we made there, in the face of a gale and snow warning. We turfed out all surplus gear and packed our sacks with food and camping kit for a campaign into the wild interior lying behind Slioch.

My friend Iain and I believe that you should break from the tyranny of the motor car whenever you can, and now with food for four days, camp kit, rope and ice-axes, we abandoned easy ways for a path up a loch whipped into white-horses by a wind which had the merit of gusting into our backs. We needed it for the lift out of Glen Bianasdail, where the path climbs between rocky knobs to a wide cirque of green, and the first of many rickles of stones tells of a population now gone. The whole length of Loch Maree is sporting estate owned by three landlords.

We had fixed our minds on a little bay, shown on the map, as a possible place of shelter. 'Look, look!' exclaimed Iain with some excitement when it lay 300 ft below us, hemmed by knolls of oak trees growing right down to the edge of the loch. 'Perfect,' I registered gladly as we sank down in the north corner of this heaven-sent shelter.

Whatever the weather brought, we were dry, and in possession of the kind of place that cannot be reached by any motor car. Tucked into our sleeping bags by 9 p.m. we were dead men until wakened by the songs of blackbirds, chaffinches and trilling wrens. The time was 7.30 and there was not a cloud in the pale sky. So without getting out of my warm bag I lit the stove and put on water to boil. We had breakfast in bed and were on our way into the sunshine by 9 a.m., leaving the tent standing with a little rucksack inside it, containing enough food for two meals.

A varied mile and a half of green path lay ahead of us, exciting for the way it threaded the silver birches and oaks, revealing a herd of wild goats one moment, and Highland ponies the next, while over our heads went more than a hundred snow buntings, making their own little blizzard of white wings as they swirled about in a torrent of tinkling sound.

Less than two miles ahead now was the place with the ominous name of Furnace, site of the earliest known ironworks in the Highlands, dating back to around 1600. Seven other iron furnaces were later sited around Loch Maree until 'the trees were all spent'. The oaks which were used up were the most westerly in Scotland, and what is left today is a remnant.

Just how extensive the woodland cover must have been we saw when we left the loch to take a short cut over the ridge into the great corrie formed between Slioch and Ben Lair, where Loch Garbhaig sends down the Furnace river through twisted rocks. We walked on decomposing roots sunk in the sphagnum bog, which bore our weight because it was frozen hard.

With the wind behind us we decided we would use its strength to help us climb Ben Lair. True it meant carrying the rucksacks over the top but we soon forgot their weight in the brilliant March sunshine giving a new-washed look to the grey rocks and winter-bleached grasses. A great moment when we breasted the summit ridge and looked across the gulf of Glen Tulacha to the rock walls of A' Mhaighdean. Down there under it was the Fionn Loch, like a vast cloud shadow, with the white spot of Carn More on its edge, the deserted house which was our destination.

For me this was return after an absence of nearly 25 years. The family of MacRaes who used to live here were my friends. Now the house is used only in the shooting season, but two sheds are left open for passing climbers, and within minutes we had the stove going for for cups of as good coffee as I am likely to taste in this lifetime. It was nectar because we had waited so long for it.

Now we turned our thoughts to the steep gully above the house, which is flanked by two great crags of bulging gneiss. We should have been tired, but the challenge of the *arête* forming the left ledge of the east face could not be resisted, even if it meant being overtaken by darkness. In half an hour we were roping-up for a sparkling climb on mostly vertical rock, arriving on top of the buttress in moonlight, while westwards over the vast greyness of the Fionn Loch a touch of fire still remained in the sky.

Carefully we picked our way down in the darkness to the shed, where we secured the door against the icy rattle of the wind, which was gale-force by morning. It put paid to our plan to explore the wild crags of the Gorm Loch Mor, but it was by that route we climbed out to the ridge crest of Beinn Tharsuinn Chaol to descend to Loch Fhada. Now we were grinding into the wind, until we swung south on an 800-ft climb which brought us back to Furnace and our camp, where we were soon unearthing our soup, steak and quarter-loaf for an eagerly anticipated meal.

An almost overpowering warmth in our arctic-quality sleeping bags that night told us the air had gone mild. The change had come at last. The loch was calm and the sky had lost its steely quality, so we used our last day to climb Slioch by its north cliffs which have a steeply pinnacled character. On a previous trip we had been defeated while trying to explore them.

That day we had everything our way. We were fit, and an 800-ft tower which had looked difficult proved to be just a scramble. It made the perfect finish to out little campaign, giving us mighty views of Liathach and Ben Eighe towering above masses of low clouds drifting about their corries. It was time we were going, for we had eaten our last slice of bread. On the trudge back to the car we met the first heavy rain of the trip just as we were within a mile of its shelter.

Loch Maree takes its modern name from the wooded island called Eilein Maruighe which became famous as a place of pilgrimage through St Maelrubha of Applecross, who built a cell or chapel here. The older name of the loch was Loch Ewe, as is indicated by the name of the village of Kinlochewe at its head. Loch Ewe is, of course, the sea loch into which Loch Maree empties by the short River Ewe. The run of spring salmon and autumn sea trout entering by the short river makes Loch Maree one of the best fishing lochs in Scotland and the hotel at Talladale has a good reputation.

Walkers should consider the woodland track, which begins at Slattadale opposite the main mass of islands in the widest part of Loch Maree, keeping fairly close to the shore at first, then crossing behind a craggy hill to come down on the main road a mile and a half from Poolewe. May is the time to do this traverse, when the natural oaks and birches are at their most brilliant greens and yellow, curtaining the grey crags of Creag Mhor, and all round you is a torrent of bird song from redstarts, tree pipits, and willow and wood warblers. Look out too for redwings, which have been colonizing in recent years.

The public road to Poolewe detours west from Loch Maree at Slattadale to the coast at Loch Gairloch, the right branch taking you past the fish-landing pier to the considerable village on the north arm of the bay. Tourism flourishes here, with golf course, guest houses, hotels, youth hostel and crofts offering Bed and Breakfast. The whole range of the Torridon hills form the view over the loch, usually with a foreground of hovering terns and bobbing eider ducks.

A climb over the hills eastward brings you down to Loch Ewe. Crossing that rocky moor one late September afternoon we had an unexpected flash of drama, when suddenly the whole world took on a tinge of fire. The black sky had become pink. Loch Tollie was crimson, yet we were looking not towards the sunset but away from it. Even as we shouted out our disbelief at the burning brilliance of the Carn More peaks the fire began to fade. The west was hidden from us by near hills, until we turned north to Loch Ewe and faced such a riot of gold and crimson that only the black silhouettes of headlands distinguished painted sea from sky.

Like Gairloch, Poolewe is a popular holiday village, and deservedly so, with miraculous gardens on the edge of the bay overlooking the best peaks in Wester Ross, a place moreover where you can listen to the reeling of dunlin at dawn and dusk, watch black-throated divers or perhaps see great northern divers which have bred on this coast, while east and west are remote headlands spattered with good fishing lochs.

Relatives of mine who rented a croft for a fortnight at Cove, on the west side of Loch Ewe, brought up a load of books from London, expecting to find the evenings of late September a bit long. None were read. Between chatting to the sociable crofters and exploring the neighbourhood, the days had melted into nights and London life seemed more remote than this more natural world.

They blessed the inspiration of the moment that had brought them to Morag, when they answered an advertisement in a Sunday newspaper of a croft to let. Morag, a widow, lived at the north side of the house, busily trying to get in late sheaves of oats between milking the cow twice a day. But now and then she would look in with a plate of warm scones and pancakes, or a basin of boiled shellfish; or just to see that there were plenty of peats for the fire.

They saw too at Inverasdale nearby the tiny factory that turns out parts for lathes, screws, spindles, rings, etc., which are so valuable that each ton produced is worth about £1,000. Set up by industrialist Mr John Rollo twenty years ago to help arrest depopulation, it employs only three men but has been a definite success.

The NATO base across the loch at Aultbea is the largest employer of labour, and a valuable factor in keeping alive the crofting tradition here, since the land by itself is insufficient. For a vivid picture of what this country was like last century, Osgood Mackenzie's *A Hundred Years in the Highlands* is classic reading.

Osgood was the creator of Inverewe Gardens, which now draws over 100,000 visitors each year. I have a personal debt to Mackenzie, for he made me look closely at a landscape and a society which I took for granted. Here was a man who died when I was eight years old, yet he was on terms of intimacy with a grand uncle who had served under the Earl of Cromartie who fought at Culloden. That general, 'Fighting Jack' John Mackenzie, died in 1900, thus Culloden, and all the terrible events that sprang from it, ceased to become ancient history to me.

Osgood's grandfather, Sir Hector Mackenzie, had known the time when thousands of wild roses grew everywhere on his property, and game was so plentiful that vermin was never trapped. The gamekeeper was really employed as a game killer. But in Osgood's time the woods had been burned and the hills over-grazed. Profits from sheep had declined, and the wealthy industrialists were putting their money into Highland estates for deer stalking, grouse shooting and salmon fishing.

Mackenzie was himself a blood-thirsty shot like his father before him. Killing was one of the joys of his life. The other was gardening, and his monument is Inverewe House, which he built on a former sea beach and around it created a rival to Kew. First of all he had to create shelter, which meant waiting 20 years for trees he planted to grow up, then he began his miracle. In 60 years he proved to the world that the north-west Highlands are not Siberia though they happen to share the same latitude. Shelter—and the Gulf Stream—seems to make anything possible, and Mackenzie could boast that any plant which will grow in the open in Britain will do well here.

I remember one exceptionally cold spring when there was no growth of grass anywhere and the hills were colourless after the winter rains and frosts. But in Inverewe you stepped into another world of humid little valleys, screened by tall pines and vivid rhododendrons crowding round a magnolia, large pink cups high overhead against green larches and blue sky. It was a shock afterwards to walk out on to sour moor on the north side.

Visitors from outlandish places on both sides of the equator are always thrilled to find the plants they know at home blooming vigorously here. Personally I was delighted to see on that spring visit little dwarf daffodils of vivid yellow, with leaves hardly broader than blades of grass, which I had last seen in the Atlas Mountains of Morocco.

The object of that particular visit had been to take some panoramic photographs for the National Trust for Scotland indicator viewpoint at Tournaig, on the high road between Aultbea and Poolewe. For this I needed absolute clarity to identify every peak, and it was a few days before a change of wind brought the conditions required. But it was worth waiting for when all the greatest ranges of Wester Ross stood clear and snow-capped from the wilds of A' Mhaighdean to the jostling summits of Torridon.

A new prospect opens out when you drop over the other side down to Gruinard Bay with its crofts, pink sandy coves, and rivers emptying from the wilderness behind. You feel this is the kind of place where people were meant to live, facing out over a great sweep of sea, spattered with islets. Yet the total naturalness of Gruinard conceals something sinister. Look at the island which occupies a mile of the bay. No one is allowed to land there, because it was used for germ-warfare experiments in the war and remains contaminated. The danger is of anthrax and the price of trespass could be an ugly death. Warning notices are posted.

Fifteen miles due north across the water in Coigach lies Rieff, beyond the Summer Isles, but to reach it by road you have to come away inland and turn the double bite which the sea makes into the hills. Round from Gruinard, the first bite is Little Loch Broom with Dundonnel at its head and above it, Liathach's only rival, An Teallach.

This Torridonian sandstone mountain deserves thorough exploration, even if you only penetrate the two great rock recesses known as A' Ghlas Thuill and Loch Toll an Lochain, on the Dundonnel side of the mountain, and approachable through pines and tumbling waterfalls. The hilltrack that goes to Strath na Shellag is the one I would recommend you to take, for an easy climb to over 1,000 ft by rock slabs and birches, until you strike off for Loch Toll an Lochain.

The corrie is an impressively barren place, hemmed by mounds of morainic spoil with fierce pinnacles thrusting above the loch to the sky. Yet the summit traverse of the eleven tops is surprisingly easy, including the best bit of the ridge by Sgurr Fiona and over Lord Berkeley's Seat to Corrag Bhuidhe. It is at its best when there is a play of shifting mist, when black fangs materialize out of space, and far below you can glimpse the Summer Isles flashing green on the sunlit sea. Cross-country walkers descending into the Strath na Shellag can continue on through the hills to Carn More on the Fionn Loch. To thoroughly explore this roadless country between Loch Maree and Loch Broom needs many, many visits and nights out in the sleeping bag.

Nobody lives permanently in this block of country. It is too wild, yet Strath Beag above Dundonnell seems so civilized, with its big parks and fine trees. The good broad road is a big temptation to speed past without looking closely at it. Arriving here once by walking from Loch Maree, I had merely to cross the hill and signal the ferry to be taken across Loch Broom to Ullapool. The motorist heading there has to climb over a wild moor to gain the Garve–Ullapool road where the river has cut a spectacular gorge at Corriesalloch.

The National Trust for Scotland have built a lay-by just west of the main road, to enable visitors to leave their cars and walk on to the bridge over the narrow gorge and see the great column of white water that plunges 200-ft into it. The gorge itself is a glacial melt-water channel, and was originally fed by a reservoir of ice, whose gushing stream cut the box canyon.

The drop from here to the sea is a journey into fertility as you come back into the world of trees and fields. You are more surely back to the land of tourism too, for Ullapool is one of the most thriving holiday villages in Scotland, and deserves to be, with the kind of situation it has on a sheltered sea loch with a constant coming and going of fishing boats, for this is one of the principal herring-landing ports on the west coast.

Ullapool, like Oban, was built by the British Fisheries Society in 1788 to exploit the plentiful supply of herrings in the Minch. But the bounty did not last. Today it is mostly east coast fishermen who land the catches, and Ullapool itself lives mainly by tourism, offering plenty of organized activities, sea-angling being something of a specialty.

Coigach is the name given to that part of Loch Broom parish which contains the north shore of this biggest sea loch in the north-western Highlands. Along that coast lies Achiltibuie, which can be reached on foot from Strathkanaird by a fine path known as 'The Rock', and on my first visit I did just that, returning over the top of Ben More Coigach for a view which revealed to me that Loch Broom was a frontier between two distinctive types of country.

To the south, the thronging mountains were ranges of jumbled summits of almost equal height. Northward, by contrast, each peak stood alone, heaving up dramatically, and having a dignity out of all proportion to its size: Cul Mor, Stac Polly, Suilven and Canisp. West of me stretched a ragged coast of fjords and wide bays. North between the monolithic peaks, was the low ground of Coigach, peppered with rocks and lochans.

The easiest way to penetrate Coigach is to take the fast north road out of Ullapool and swing west at Drumrunie on single track along Loch Lurgain. Get into a passing place and look up at the astonishing bristles of Stac Polly and at the rough grain of the country opposite across the Loch.

Across the shoulder of Stac Polly lies Loch Sionascaig, in the Inverpolly Nature Reserve, and a good path leads over to it from a point near the cottage of Linneraineach. It makes the perfect introduction to a landscape of remnant peaks of ancient rocks, denuded by ice-age glaciers, which have left innumerable hollows now occupied by lochs, and thinly clothed in places by birch, hazel, oak, willow, aspen, pine, holly and juniper.

Little of this forest remains today. The evidence lies in the peat, where the trees fell when the climate worsened. Some tree cover did remain in the drier, better-drained areas, until man began increasingly exploiting it for war and peace. His inroads were light, however, until the large-scale introduction of sheep 200 years ago when heather and grass were burned to increase growth, resulting in an impoverished top soil as nutritious plants were replaced by coarser grass and wet-loving vegetation.

The Nature Conservancy took over Inverpolly to try to recreate these woodlands, after studying the scrubby fragments which remain. Strangely enough, the tree-loving long-eared owl still nests here, and in the tumbled rocks live pine martens and wildcats. Amongst the birches redstarts, willow warblers and treepipits nest. Walking is difficult in this rough country except on the paths.

But the first time I ever came here was direct through the hills from Elphin on the Sutherland border, over trackless ground with a heavy pack—worth it for the delight of pitching camp beneath Cul Mor on an alp of birches above a bay of yellow sand on Loch Sionascaig, with 'drumming' snipe and curlews shrilling all about us.

We set off at five o'clock that evening for the top of Stac Polly, choosing a great rib of warm sandstone which proved exhilaratingly severe, then came the traverse along the edge of the porcupine quills of the summit pinnacles. This western seaboard has been described as being Norwegian in character. It is true enough, when all the bays are silver and the islands are silhouettes, and inland stretches a bare waste like the arctic tundra. That was how we saw it that night.

Next day we took in the two summits, Cul Mor and Cul Beag, and walked out to the Loch Lurgain road to catch the mail bus on the morning after. That bus goes to Achiltibuie, where the great explorer Tom Longstaff wrote his classic book *This My Voyage*. This is how he sums up his feeling for his last home.

I have written this book in Coigach, the extreme north-west extremity of Wester Ross, nearly 100 miles north of the Great Glen. A true mountain country, aloof from the Lowlands but within sight and sound of the sea. There is spaciousness here. Light and colour are always changing on hill and water. One is conscious of the continual movement of nature, in the sea, in the running water and in the wind that drives the clouds before it in procession across the sky. In winter, Atlantic gales and furious volleys of rain or sudden splintering hail keep the air alive and exciting . . . . An exciting land.

So I have come back there to live.

Local people have the same feeling for this landscape. One I spoke to on my last visit was Donnie MacLeod, the Achiltibuie postman. He fishes lobsters in his spare time and is a keen crofter. He had been out to sea at 7.30 a.m. had done some work on his sheep, and at 11.30 a.m. was going in to have an hour skin-diving before starting his postal round at 3 p.m.

'What we fear on this peninsula is that we've been written off, that our houses are going to pass to the 'white settlers' as we are forced to leave to get work in industry on the Moray Firth. But we like it here, if we could get a living. There are a dozen young men like myself, who have to work on the road, or a distance away in order to live here. If we just had one small industry here it would make all the difference.'

We talked about the owner occupation of crofts, but he had a divided mind. He voiced a fear that in the end it would lead to the resale at a profit, and the future crop could all too easily become camp and caravan sites.

Donnie's wise old mother told me of the times, forty years ago, when every house was lived in by a crofter fisherman. 'Once we were so busy here that the day wasn't long enough for you, cutting, stacking and carrying the peats, milking the cows at ten o'clock of a summer night, working the hay and getting in the harvest. Nobody cuts peats now. Some don't even keep hens. It's all coals and electricity. We had good ceilidhs, too. I think we were happier in the old days before the tourists. The place is changing too fast.'

It was changing so fast that when I went to the most northerly crofting township at Rieff I found such a congestion of campers that the crofters had asked Mrs Longstaff, the owner, to intervene. The wife of the explorer explained to me that the camping situation had steadily been getting worse, but she didn't want to do anything about it until the crofters requested it themselves.

'We've talked it over, and decided that anyone who asks for permission will be directed to one of four sites. And when these are full up, there will be an overflow site until they can move on. It's simply a question of physical space and sanitation.'

To go north up the coast by road you have to return east to Loch Bad a Ghaill and take the Lochinver road past the green oasis of Strathpolly where the Nature Conservancy warden lives beneath a rock, among birches loud with the singing of siskins in the spring. Here in the dark you can sometimes hear the pine martens quarrelling like cats, and sometimes they come to the bird table for scraps.

Sutherland lies just ahead, signposted by the weird rock-stack of Suilven.

CHAPTER TEN

Sutherland

Inchnadamph—Kylesku—Scourie—Durness— Cape Wrath—Tongue—the Reay Forest

Of all the country we have looked at so far, none is richer in reward for the discerning visitor than this most north-westerly part of the Scottish mainland. Sparsely inhabited, incredibly bleak in bad weather, rocky, boggy and with innumerable lochs, it is the nearest scenic approach to an arctic landscape we have in Britain, even to the plants and the scrub birch. Legendary amongst fishermen, botanists, ornithologists, geologists, and speleologists, it is also the land where the destructive hand of man is most obvious, since this is the classic ground of the clearances. Human history and natural history march hand in hand.

The more you know about Sutherland, the more you will enjoy it. So when you drive north out of Ullapool, make a stop at Knockan visitor centre where a big effort has been made by the Nature Conservancy to interpret the countryside for you. The three-quarters of a mile Knockan Cliff nature trail should be walked if the weather is at all kind, for it was here that geologists saw before their faces the evidence of how the mountain ranges of the world were formed.

That evidence is in the layers of rock which have over-ridden each other, with bottom layers of ancient rocks pushed on top of younger unaltered sediments. At Knockan the movement occurred 400 million years ago, twisting and folding eight layers of different strata.

This force began at Whiten Head in north Sutherland, rippled over the Torridon hills, in a thrust of schist, spending itself in Skye in a breaker 120 miles long by 12 miles wide in places. This was at the time of the Caledonian mountain-building period, and geologists call it the Moine Thrust. So Knockan Cliff is of world geological importance and the carefully written pamphlet explains the rocks, the plants, the general natural history and background.

The Inverpolly motor trail booklet will also enhance your future journeys. North of Knockan, Elphin crofting township lies just ahead, so strikingly green that it is a revelation of the immediate effect of limestone outcropping. The best view of Suilven is from here, not the rounded haystack seen from Lochinver, but twin fangs of rock leaping from the watery moor, challenging to any mountaineer, yet hardly more than as easy scramble when you get there. Ahead lies further moorland, then green grass, birches, and a feeling of arrival as you come into Inchnadamph, with Loch Assynt before you, and above it lumpy Quinag and the quartzite summit of Conival.

It was from Inchnadamph I climbed all the hills in this neighbourhood, wandering up the Traligall in May, on grey pavements which were natural rock gardens of alpine plants, looking at the Allt nan Uamh and the famous bone caves where the remains of the earliest people to colonize Scotland have been found, together with the bones of animals which roamed these hills then: brown bear, northern lynx, reindeer and lemmings. The ptarmigan bones indicate it was widespread at low levels in these more arctic times.

The Traligall Burn and the Allt nan Uamh offer the greatest pot-holing challenge in Scotland, with underground passages in the limestone which are only now being discovered. On Ben More above them, the gneiss reaches the very top, at 3,273 ft, a height record for the oldest rock. From up there you can look from the Hebrides to the Cairngorms, but it is the uniqueness of Assynt at your feet which is compelling, wave crests of grey gneiss trapping hundreds of minute lochans in their troughs, and above them peaks of pink sandstone and capping quartzite like snow. In the light of a fine sunset the bare-rock landscape glows with the changing colours.

Go over the rather featureless peak of Canisp, traverse on, and go for Suilven, if you would enjoy everything that makes Assynt: the bedrock of gneiss, the lochans, the singing meadow pipits, the cries of greenshank, blue flowers of butterwort, pink lousewort, yellow tormentil, starry saxifrages, roseroot and many another. That was how it was on my first visit, too heat hazy for really spectacular views.

I returned on another May day to try a rock climb on the big butt-end of the 'Grey Castle' which faces Lochinver. The climbing here is steep and technically hard and we consumed hours of time working a way up. The reward was to arrive on the summit at the best time of evening, when every gully was picked out with shadow and every quartz summit gleamed softly in alpenglow. Over the blue dots of lochans we looked from the Outer Isles to the Cuillin, and the red light was fading from the peaks as we crossed Canisp to reach the tent towards midnight.

Loch Assynt, pointing north-west, occupies six miles of an ancient valley and has a reputation for being stormy amongst fishermen out by boat from Inchnadamph Hotel. The numerous bays and islands under the fine peak of Quinag give it scenic variety, and Ardvreck Castle ruins are worth a visit, for it was here the great Montrose was betrayed by the Macleods of Assynt and handed over to be taken to the Grassmarket in Edinburgh and executed in 1650. The price on Montrose's head was £20,000 and it is the only act in Highland history of a clansman betraying another for gold. Retribution caught up, however, with the restoration of the monarchy, when the Mackenzies acting for Charles II harried all Assynt and held it for a hundred years.

West beyond Loch Assynt lies the busy fishing port of Lochinver. Our own route for now keeps the new road north of Skiag Bridge, climbing over the shoulder of Quinag and coming down to the sea at Loch Cairnbawn. From the summit of this road two fine possibilities open up, one the ascent of Quinag, 2,653 ft, on the west, the other a trip over the Bealach a' Bhurich to see the biggest waterfall in Scotland. For either of these trips you need about three hours.

Bog cotton was tossing in the wind and Loch Ganvich was a surface race of water as we parked the car and took the rocky path for the big waterfall. Making height easily we climbed into a corrie of little lochans cradled in sparkling quartzite, and above our heads white fleecy clouds scudded over the top of Ben More.

Over the Bealach—a pass in the ridge—we now followed a rightward path, stopping in our tracks when an eagle came swooping low, skimming the ground at no more than 100 ft, a portion of hare dangling from one yellow talon. We lost sight of the bird as it swung into a dense mat of birches clinging to the steep rocks. Our own track maintained a high line to avoid the rocks, but hearing the booming sound of the fall below us, we struck down at the first burn. The distance is less than a mile from the top of the pass.

A short scramble, and in front of us was what we sought, a white

34   *Wildest Ross: from A' Mhaighdean looking down on the Gorm Loch. Background peaks lie across hidden Loch Maree*

spout of water curving through the air, disappearing out of sight in a mist of rainbow. Down a little further, and now we could see where the single column crashed on the rocks and divided into twin tresses, meeting again to form a cascade in a final fling, total height 650 ft. Locally the fall is known as the Maiden's Tresses, but the Gaelic name is Eas Coul Aulin.

How does it compare to the Fall of Glomach? On the scale of beauty I would hand the prize to the Eas Coul Aulin because of its open situation and variety of outlook to the head of Loch Glencoul and the green strath running inland beneath the grey rampart of Ben More Assynt. But it has nothing of the overpowering weight of compressed waters hurtling into the gloomy Glomach ravine. You can stand back at the Eas Coul Aulin. You are not perched among the waters as on that giddy pinnacle at Glomach.

The summit of Quinag from the roadside at Loch Ganvich is a lift of only 1,800 ft. A fit man will climb it in just over an hour, and from up there stretches the finest view in Sutherland, Loch Assynt on one side, Loch Cairnbawn on the other, westward the indented coast of Eddrachillis Bay, and eastward the grey peaks of Reay dropping to the coast of Cape Wrath.

That was how I had it on Quinag one memorable May day when the eye could range from the Torridon peaks to the Cuillin of Skye and up past the hills of Harris to the Butt of Lewis, then to North Rona, and the sandy bays of Oldshore.

To go north up the Sutherland coast from Inchnadamph means crossing Loch Cairnbawn by free ferry, something of a bottleneck in summer. The tourist who is just 'out for a run' should resist the temptation to take the coast road.

Quinag is at the eastern end of a rectangle of roads, with a village at each corner, Lochinver and Inchnadamph in the south, Clachnessie and Unapool in the north. This circuit is popular with motorists, but driving is difficult, for the narrow road not only wriggles, but darts up and down notorious hills, all single track, all with blind corners, and one of them has a gradient of 1 in 4. Passing places do not abound, so care is needed round every bend of the single-track.

I write this from experience of a head-on collision near Glen Ardvar, when an ancient car came over the horizon of the hill above

35 *Liathach from Loch Clair. Built of sandstone layers and capped with Cambrian quartzite, the mountain is on a base of Lewisean gneiss, the oldest rock*

me, shot past the only passing place, leaving me the minimum of time to pull as hard left as I could. There was no time to jump clear as the oncoming car crashed into my wing and jammed hard against a stone embankment on the other side.

Locked together the cars were immovable, but I could see the driver of the other car was white-faced and shaken, and hear the hysterical cries of his wife and children. We created a considerable road block, and with the help of other drivers were prised apart. The car which crashed into me had bald tyres and brakes which had failed to hold its Midlands of England driver on the hill. Luckily, with some hammering and first aid, we could both drive away. On the advice of those who had come to our aid the Midlands man turned back after being convinced that there was worse ahead than the short distance he had travelled from Unapool.

The best bit of this coast is in fact the right angle between Lochinver and Drumbeg, and wise drivers will not try to make a circular tour of it. Better to drive direct from Inchnadamph to Lochinver and explore Achmelvich, Stoer and Clachnessie, to enjoy the sandy bays and turfy headlands which are now so popular with adventurous campers. This is a crofting fringe, full of out-of-the-way corners, where you might marvel at the persistence of the Gael in hanging on to his old way of life. Eddrachillis Bay is so spattered with tiny islets that there is said to be one for every day of the year.

Badcall Bay and the attractive village of Scourie lie north across the water, and to get to them by car means crossing on the free ferry at Kylesku. This shuttle-service runs across Loch Cairnbawn, the wide fjord whose two easterly arms are Lochs Glendhu and Glencoul in hard country, remote even for Sutherland. The road north is barren enough, but beyond the peat and ill-drained soil lies the neat-walled fields and limestone greenery of Scourie, with its loch and groves of birches.

Stay in Scourie Hotel and you can have the free fishing of 280 lochs. Climb even the smallest eminence and you will find yourself bewildered by the number of them. And you will also be thrilled by the position of the village, nestling under a rocky ridge, with green bumps of fields sloping down to the sea. The bay looks out to Lewis, and southward over the protecting ridge of the village rise the Assynt peaks, Quinag dominating because it is nearest.

Ornithologists coming to Scourie will know about the nearby Isle of Handa, now owned by the RSPB. The best way to it is by car, over a narrow hill road to Tarbert, from whose lip you look down on a quilt of unfenced fields above a bay dotted with islets. Down there I met a smiling grandmother busily knitting in the drizzle, keeping watch on a couple of cows to see they did not stray into the growing crops.

Handa lies just across the narrow strait and the boatman will take you over, wind and weather being favourable, for this is a treacherous coast. On my first visit I found the village mourning a lobsterman and his two young nephews who had drowned while tending the pots. The problem here is the strength of the surf sweeping against the rocks where the best lobsters are found. Members of the RSPB are entitled to stay overnight in the rabbit trapper's hut, which has been renovated and equipped since I last stayed in it for a few days in early summer. Conditions were exciting, with rain showers and sunshine on the Reay peaks and Cape Wrath looking a mere fraction of its 18 miles' distance over the sea.

The rise from the easterly strait to the 400-ft crown of the island is grassy peat with bog-cotton lochs, where red-throated divers and great skuas breed. But the big thrill was to arrive on the cliff edge, feel the tremendous updraught of wind, and peer down to the churning sea through a swirl of birds criss-crossing in a mad traffic rush that made you feel dizzy.

Even St Kilda does not compare with Handa for its immediate impression of sheer numbers compressed into short space, for not only have you a seabird-thronged cliff below you, but immediately in front you have the nesting tenement of the Stack of Handa occupying the inlet of the bay.

Keen-eyed bird hunters of Lewis walking round this horse-shoe in 1876 saw that a long rope stretched from one side of the bay to the other would pass over the top of the Stack of Handa. They tried out the experiment, and Donald MacDonald of Lewis decided he would be the first man ever to land on top of the stack by going out hand over hand on the rope and dropping on to its grassy top.

All went well, until his weight in the middle of the long rope caused it to sag, so that he found himself in mid-air below the top of the stack. But he managed to get a foot on the rock and climb the last section unaided, after which he sent basket after basket of birds and eggs to his companions across the gulf. This was the account given to me by the boatman who had taken me over to Handa.

Now I could see the proof that the Lewisman had been there, in the wooden stakes they had left on top as a challenge to local men to recover them. Nobody did, until 1967 when Dr Tom Patey repeated the feat, using the same technique and finding the same problem of sag. With modern jumar clamps, however, he was able to climb the rope to the grassy top of the stack. He told me of his most anxious moment, when a razorbill settled on the rope as he was dangling, and began sawing away at it with its bill! Since Patey's ascent, the stack has been climbed direct from the sea in a piece of very severe modern cragsmanship.

The ruins of the former crofting township on Handa are at the south-easterly corner of the island, rickles of dry-stone above narrow strips of green reverting to bog cotton. The people who lived here were not 'cleared' as were so many in Sutherland. They were induced to go to Canada when the potato disease made their self-supporting life impossible, about twenty years before the Lewismen made their climb. The twelve families who eked a living from Handa must have been tough to survive on the produce of such a small exposed island where, tradition tells, the oldest widow was always appointed Queen.

From Scourie the road to the north swings eastward to Laxford Bridge, on the main road between Lairg and Durness. This is the edge of the Reay Forest, whose peaks you might think are reminiscent of shale-bings or spoilheaps, Arkle and Foinaven, bare and grassless to the superficial glance. But the deer stalking here is some of the best in Scotland, and the salmon fishing is of legendary quality.

To explore the interior of the Reay is impossible by car, so meantime we shall go north on the Durness road, round the head of Loch Laxford by the wilderness of grey and pink gneiss to Loch Chalhaidh, and take the track which leads to Ardmore. You can go so far by car, but after that you have to walk four miles to where the path ends at an oasis of birches and croft houses perched high above the sea. On the shore below lies the remotest museum in Scotland.

It is a shed containing the rowing boat which took Capt. John Ridgeway and fellow-paratrooper Sgt. Chay Blyth across the Atlantic from Cape Cod to the Aran Islands of Ireland. The idea came to

John Ridgeway in his croft here as he was shaving and listening to the morning news on the radio. He told me how it came about.

'I was trying to be a crofter on $2\frac{1}{2}$ acres of arable and a half share of 2,000 acres of hill. We got the croft because it's four miles from any road. 'We' includes my wife for we'd just got married. So we both had to work that summer of 1964. That morning, as I was shaving, I heard on the wireless that a man was going to row the Atlantic and was looking for a partner. I tried to join him but he had got fixed up. So I decided to race him if I could find the right companion.

'You've seen the boat in the shed. It felt even smaller in the water'. Terror, hunger, luck and prayer were the ingredients of that epic row, which lasted 92 days. It was during that frightful journey that Ridgeway got another idea, to found an adventure school for youngsters on the arm of Loch Laxford by his croft. 'I felt it would be a worthwhile way of life, and it would enable me to pass on the skills which have given me so much pleasure in life.'

He drew up the detailed plan for his adventure school in a yacht called *English Rose* IV when he competed in the Golden Globe race, sailing single-handed round the world. Knocked out of the race in Brazil by a TV boat which had got too close and damaged him, he came home to make his adventure school a reality.

The timber building further up the loch is a second-hand factory which he bought in Dingwall, transporting it here and re-erecting it with a workforce of three, one of them the crofter next door. To support the 92-ft building, 500 concrete blocks had to be made, each weighing 40 lbs. Showers, washbasins, drying room—all were installed without help from tradesmen.

What Ridgeway imparts to those who go on his course—and they are not confined to the young—is the pleasure to be had from doing worthwhile things, sailing, canoeing, climbing, hill-walking, camping and 'expeditioning'. The aim is not 'character building' but enthusiasm for living.

'Thataway, that is my view,' said John, waving his hand over a twisted ocean of rock crests to the grey rampart of Arkle and Foinaven, whose quartzite desert was gleaming white one moment and dimming purple the next. Subtle changes were taking place around us, as wind ripples changed the colour of the lochs and near rocks took on a hue of pink. 'You should see it in winter, that's when I like it best.

It's even more colourful,' interposed Mrs Ridgeway. Large-eyed and dressed in a mini-skirt, she looked like a schoolgirl, but cooks for 40 in a small kitchen.

Back on the main road to Rhiconich, you should go west if you would see another delightful road-end, where the bleakness of Loch Inchard gives way to the sandy machair and bays between bold headlands of Torridonian sandstone where the Atlantic breakers burst. Tracks lead down to the scattered crofts, and lose themselves on the greensward, but please do not drive around over the turf in your car for it is the flowers which make this a place to treasure, the rich variety of orchis growing with mountain avens and even *Primula Scotica*.

You can walk to remote Sandwood Bay from here, on a peat track dangerously soft for a car, so do not try to take yours. The solitude of this atmospheric loch should be won the hard way. Notice the slender pinnacle of Am Buachaille, which juts vertically out of the sea on the approach to Sandwood Bay. It was explored and climbed by Dr Tom Patey in the late '6os in his great spate of stack climbing. Alas, this outstanding Alpinist and greatest Scottish mountain explorer fell to his death from another Sutherland stack as he roped off after making its first ascent.

Half-a-dozen miles along the coast protrudes the high headland of Cape Wrath, which may sound appropriate for the rough waters which collide on its vertical rocks, but the Norse name was *Hvarf*, which means turning point. The Gaelic of it is *Parph*, and is given to the whole upper part of the peninsula. No path goes north to it from Sandwood.

The motorist must return the way he has come, past the sheltered bays of Kinlochbervie and its busy fish-landing port. From here the lorries start out on their big journey to Aberdeen, and buses and cars take east-coast fishermen back to their villages for the weekend. Kinlochbervie has become increasingly important as a fish-landing port over the years, but the roads are still a trial to all those who have to drive back and fore.

From Rhiconich the route to the south follows the lochs of More, Merkland and Shin to Lairg, which is the hub of the Sutherland road system. From Lairg railway station, buses operate to Scourie, Durness and Tongue. But except on the indented coast, there are no cross-country connections between these single-track roads.

Back to Rhiconich on the A 838, Durness is only 13 miles north-east, on a road that climbs past the extremity of Foinaven, and crosses the bleak watershed to join the River Dionard emptying into the Kyle of Durness. This peaty and featureless stretch is the perfect foil for the green revelation of the Durness limestone and the cheery houses of the straggling village which has waters on three sides of its peninsula, all with delightful sandy bays.

West of Durness on the Kyle, at the Cape Wrath Hotel, you can take the ferry across and connect with a mini-bus for a trip to the lighthouse. Given a fine day, the chance to walk the ten miles east back to the ferry should not be missed. Walking along these cliff tops, nothing but the ocean and floating ice lies between you and the North Pole.

I had the good luck to be here one cold May day of north wind and snow showers when the fury of the battering waves made you shrink back from the cliff edge. We could enjoy it more at Kervaig Bay just over two miles east of the lighthouse, where a sandy curve is broken by rock stacks. Here you could sit back and watch the bursting explosions of spume, mushrooming almost over the stacks in a crash and suck of sound. The noise echoed back not only from the stacks but from a rising rampart of Torridonian sandstone which reaches a height of 600 ft and is the most impressive sea cliff of its kind. It is called the Clo Mor.

We climbed up there, finding the walking easy on short turf ablaze with seapinks, and now and again we would wriggle to the edge to peer down on the layers of sea birds buzzing back and fore like bees and sending up such a volume of wild cries that it sounded above the boom and blast of the waves. In green gullies we had puffins sitting almost beside us.

Clo Mor seemed invulnerable, but alas, this greatest sea bird-nesting cliff on the Scottish mainland has suffered a sad diminution of sea birds of recent years, due to the use of the sea area for a bombing range, and also to oil pollution.

Durness, population about 400, thrives on tourism these days with craft centre and new hotel in the old RAF camp at Balnakiel. The big fields show that it is farming not crofting that is practised here. The rainfall of less than 40 inches a year deserves to make it a prosperous place, but I am concerned at the proposal to build a tourist road along the west side of the Kyle of Durness, linking it to Cape Wrath. If there was a population out there requiring the road as a social need, I could see the point, but no one lives permanently on this peninsula except lighthouse keepers. The rewards of Cape Wrath should demand some effort, even if it is only crossing on the ferry to catch the mini-bus.

One mile or so along the road from Durness is the natural arch of the famous Smoo Cave, where the stream, crashing into darkness, disappears into a hole. Climb down to sea level and you are confronted by the big natural arch of the cave and the emergent stream, but the interior waterfall is invisible except to potholers braving the inner pools. Eastward from here you look across the mouth of Loch Eriboll to Whiten Head. Notice the twin rock stacks below that cliff. It was from one of these that Dr Tom Patey fell to his death, when he separated from his abseiling rope.

The main road has to loop south round the exceptionally deep water of Loch Eriboll past the little white church which looks on the most splendid aspect of the peaks of Reay, showing a craggier front and more peaky aspect than from the western approach. We shall go across country to them by a path from Strath More. Meantime we go north-east and cross the foot of Loch Hope, pause and take a look at the most northerly peak over 3,000 ft in Scotland, Ben Hope.

Notice how close the foot of Loch Hope is to the bay of Eriboll, with only a short river separating the fresh water from the salt. When King Hakon of Norway was making for Cape Wrath to sail his fleet to the Clyde he anchored here and in an eclipse of the sun saw an ill omen for himself which proved all too true.

Loch Hope is not bleak, nor is it isolated, for a narrow motoring road runs its length and continues by Strathmore to join the A 836 at Altnahara Inn, on the main road from Lairg to Tongue. Meantime we shall maintain our easterly direction from Loch Eriboll, climbing over a peat moor to the Kyle of Tongue beneath the hunched peaks of Ben Loyal.

Tongue village lies across the water, in a sandy situation like the Kyle of Durness, and this village too is an attractive tourist resort. Another name is Kirkiboll, but the Gaelic Geann-T-Saile A' Mhica-oidh for it is more literal, meaning 'the head of Mackay's salt water'. since this was a seat of the Mackay, Lord Reay, whose name is

perpetuated in the Reay Forest and in the name of Dounreay, which was another of his seats.

Tongue House was built by the chief of the Mackays in 1678 and occupies a sheltered position near the shore. Castle Varrich goes back a lot further, to Norse times, but the history of its ruins is lost in time. The charming situation of Tongue is best appreciated from a wild hill top like Ben Loyal, looking down from rock to peat, and beyond it the yellow sands of the Kyle with green woods catching the sun against blue sea. That was how it looked to me on my first view of it on a late evening after a black rainstorm.

Tongue is almost as far east as we go on this survey, but it is worth going just a bit further to the Borgie estuary to look at the grassy outlines of the old village of Lon, dating back to the Norse settlers of the ninth century, it is thought. Indeed it is possible that the crofting system practised by the Norsemen remained unchanged until the Clearances and the coming of sheep. On the coast the dispossessed kept to the old system which still persists today on this north coast.

In the terrible history of the evictions, it is saddening to reflect that the worst horrors were perpetrated in the name of 'improvement'. Even sadder to think that Lord Reay, the Mackay himself, should sell his land to this 'improver' nine years after the atrocities of 1820. The new owner was, of course, George Leveson-Gower, hated Duke of Sutherland, owner of all the land from Cape Wrath to Dornoch, from the Atlantic coast of Sutherland to the Firth of the North Sea, a total of over 1,700 square miles.

Historians treat the human problem dispassionately, using the logic of congestion and the necessity to reduce the numbers of people crowding each other out and resulting in poverty for all. Listen to Rosalind Mitchison in *A History of Scotland* published in 1970:

The intention of the Duke of Sutherland was to get the population on to the coasts to form fishing villages. The handling of this in Strathnaver by the absent landowner and a factor with a vested interest in haste was inept, and no attempt was made to help the new activity. Real hardship was caused, and more significantly, lasting bitterness, so that the Sutherland clearances have become a slogan focusing feeling against the landowning class in general.

37   The cliffs of the Sutherland coast, from Handa Island

For the clansmen, property ownership was a new concept, dating only from Culloden and the break-up of the old order. Until then, the clan chief was head of the clan, administering the land for his people through his tacksmen, but his real wealth was in the fighting men at his disposal, and no clansman dared say no if he called them out. But when the clan chiefs became owners, and fighting men were no longer of value, the too numerous vassals became a burden to the chief.

This is how John Prebble wrote of it in *The Highland Clearances*:

Once the chiefs lost their power many of them lost also any parental interest in their clansmen. During the next hundred years they continued the work of Cumberland's battalions. So that they might lease their glens and braes to sheep-farmers from the Lowlands and England, they cleared the crofts of men, women and children, using police and soldiers where necessary.

Yet it is true that many chiefs impoverished themselves trying to support an increasing number of people. Many sold out because there was no other course. The failure of the potato crop in 1846 and 1847 brought matters to a head and people were put to work building roads or supported by charitable funds raised by subscription. The second Duke of Sutherland, who succeeded an enormously rich father, is said to have spent £78,000 on relief, while continuing the ancestral work of improvement and clearance. But poverty was rife and the land slowly emptied.

But just as the value of men had declined, so did the value of sheep as the grazings became impoverished and Australian competition was being felt by 1870. The landowners were not unduly worried, for a richer form of rent had just appeared. The new rich of the industrial revolution were paying high prices for sport, and in the market to buy Highland estates where they could build lodges and shooting boxes.

The Utopian age of deer forests, which had lasted the best part of 80 years, was over by the time I arrived on the scene in the 1930s. By that time most of the wealthy aristocrats and industrialists who had built the shooting lodges had died, or were considerably poorer. But 195 deer forests still remained, occupying 3,000,000 acres, even though many of the keepers and retainers had been paid-off. In the Reay Forest of Sutherland the old magnificence of life-style still remained, and does to this day, for the Westminster Estate is one of the most prosperous in the Highlands.

The Reay Mountains cannot be driven through. They must be walked. On my first exploration of them I went from the Tongue side, by taking the train to Lairg, catching the connecting mail bus and getting off at the head of Loch Loyal with camping kit and food for a few days in my heavy rucksack. I was on embarkation leave from the army and the month was May.

Now I struck north-west along the flank of Ben Loyal, boggy going for much of the traverse, but it led me down to Loch an Dithreibh, where I knew of an empty house, in $3\frac{1}{2}$ miles. The remote situation had all I expected of it, with Ben Loyal rising craggily on one side, Ben Hope on the other, and between them the loch mirroring the yellows and reds of a gentle sunset.

I climbed both these peaks on different days, enjoying views out to the Orkneys and down to the blackness of Loch Hope. I recommend the north-western approaches to Loyal, through the high birch wood and by a hanging garden of globe flowers, tormentil, violets, willow herb, bluebells, spotted orchis and even wood sanicle. The steep slope leads on to the summit of Sgor Chaonasaid, and from then on, southward along the fine ridge, there is no climbing difficulty. Ben Hope was hardly more than a long peaty walk from this side, but from it I could see my way ahead to the Reay, by Gobernuisgach Lodge in Strathmore.

I went there in the rain next day, across trackless country, using the Allt an Achaidh burn as a guide, then striking south-west to gain Strathmore at Gobernuisgach. This is an attractively sited shooting lodge at the junction of Glen Golly of the trees and the burn of Strath Coire an Easaidh. Magnificent footpaths cross the Reay from here. That day I chose the easier of the two by the Bealach na Feith, climbing west to 1,471 ft for a dramatic view of blurred hunks of rock and pale lochs lashed by rain.

Yes, I got thoroughly soaked in that black rainstorm but it was worth it to see the world begin to solidify again as the cone of Ben Stack and the thrusting flank of Arkle leapt from a floor composed of hundreds of lochans trapped in a turmoil of hillocks stretching to Loch Laxford. Even by the standards of Assynt it was a weird twisted landscape. Four miles on I came to the first inhabited house, Airdchuillin. The kind-faced man who opened the door was the head deer stalker, John Scobbie. He took stock of me at a glance, apologized for his wife being away from home, and within minutes had the kettle on and a plate of scones and bannocks in front of me. Then wife and daughter arrived, and it was taken for granted I was staying.

In the morning I was off to climb the grey front of Arkle and follow its crest of quartzite blocks eastward, dropping to Loch an Easain Uaine, then due north, by as hard walking as you can find in Scotland, to the top of Foinaven. Now I had the whole north-west tip of Sutherland at my feet on a day as perfect as one is ever likely to find. In the clear visibility after the rains of yesterday, the contrasts of colour tempted me onwards still to Ganu Mor and Ceann Garbh, but mist formed unexpectedly and blotted out the view.

However I was not finished yet. Back along the ridge I went out east to Cnoc Duail, for I had heard about a great cliff towering a thousand feet above Loch Dionard. I was now a long way from base, but any weariness I felt was dispelled in the sight of that great quartzite wall, which I was determined to return to in peace time and climb. I did too, and had the pleasure of making the first great routes on it with my friend L. S. Lovat.

Hard walking lay ahead now, until I struck a path curling west and climbing 1,600 ft over the shoulder of Meall Horn. The evening light was low and soft. The top of the peak was only 800 ft above me, so I went up for a view sweeping from the Orkneys to the Outer Hebrides, over a glacier sea of knolls of gneiss and blue lochans. North and south I could look from the peak of Ben Hope to An Teallach in Ross.

John Scobbie is retired now, but at 72 was still the best shot in the Reay Forest as he proved on an estate shoot. He lives at Achfary now, and the new head keeper is his son Billy, who occupies the old family home. John feels he has had a very good life, serving one of the wealthiest of the old-type lairds in the Duke of Westminster, who dedicated his life to sport. And the Duke was a good master, providing well for his old servants before he died. The present Duchess carries on the tradition.

In the post-war period there has been a big emphasis on forestry and farming in the Westminster Estate, with provision for tourists too in picnic spots and lay-bys. Visitors willing to pay the fee may obtain a boat and permission to fish Loch Stack, which is so good that sometimes HM the Queen fishes there as a guest, and John has acted as a ghillie for her more than once.

Over the Western Highlands as a whole, deer stalking takes second place to fishing now. But there has been a subtle change of emphasis in recent times, due to the high price of venison, which puts the flesh first and the nobility of the antlered head second. Listen to deer stalker Henry Tegner talking about his sport:

> Nowhere else in this world except in Scotland may man today hope to climb mountains, amidst glorious scenery and shoot a stag by fair hill-stalking. The hunter who takes to the hills to stalk a red deer goes to the places that are changeless. The love of the hills is inexplicable and to many of us their attraction is irresistible; we shall continue to hunt the dun-brown deer in their fastnesses, till such time as we are physically incapacitated.

Yet, just as the defeated people of the glens multiplied faster in the post-Culloden period, because they accepted a lower and lower standard of living based on the potato, the red deer multiplied, too, beyond the capacity of the land to support good stock. After they had been banished to the mountains by the destruction of their natural forest habitat, deer stalking, with the modern rifle, for the trophy turned out to be the best way of producing too many deer on too little ground.

Nowadays it is accepted that deer have to be controlled for their own good, as well as that of farmers, foresters and crofters, since hunger makes them marauders. The modern outlook is that deer are wild animals which have to be managed, for sport as well as food, with the first subsidizing the second. An official Red Deer Commission employing six professional deer stalkers and a field officer tackles the job of marauding animals and does continuous census work with the help of local stalkers. Herds are being managed, culled annually at a figure of roughly one-sixth of the total herd, which keeps the deer population constant and is true conservation in action.

Looking backwards to the beginning of the nineteenth century there was no such thing as deer stalking. Until that time the method of killing was by hunting with armies of men and deerhounds. Dukes, earls and kings participated, driving the animals to a pre-arranged spot and killing as many as possible for venison. By 1682 deer were so scarce on the ground that a law was passed prohibiting the sale of venison for seven years. That the animals held on during the next 150 years of land abuse shows their resilience as a species. For them the age of the deer forest came just in time.

For the people living on the land the sporting era was another alien land use which could offer a future to only a few in work as grouse beaters, ghillies, deer stalkers, gamekeepers and house servants.

The economic problems of the Western Highlands in modern times has been revealed in the text of this book. But two vital things occurring at this moment are likely to change the pattern. The first and most challenging is the discovery of North Sea oil and the role of the Western Highlands in its development. The second is entry to the European Common Market and the fact that much of Scotland is a région périphérique and could qualify for grants from the Community farm guarantee fund.

But first let us question whether oil is indeed a boon for the Western Highlands. Consider the Drumbuie platform construction site, so much desired by Mowlem and Taylor Woodrow, who planned to use the croftland and the adjacent deep water of Port Cam facing Skye, so that when completed the giant platforms could be floated direct to the Shetlands with no problems of shallows.

Opposition from the National Trust for Scotland and the Drumbuie crofters, amongst others, defeated the project after a long and costly public inquiry. John Gordon, the Applecross postman, put the following plea to me: 'I trust if you can put in a word against the Port Cam development at Drumbuie you will do so. What the Highlands needs is a spread of small works all over the land, not major undertakings in one place. I'm against it as I am a Lochalsh man, and have a house and croft at Duirnish.'

The local community were divided about the whole business, and the Government played safe, by turning down the Drumbuie application as being too big, but giving the go-ahead for a smaller platform building yard across the water at Loch Kishorn under the Bealach nam Bo. It was a white-washing operation, for within less than a year the £130,000 Kishorn development had escalated into a £5 million enterprise as the £165 million Ninian Platform, the biggest in the world, got underway.

The pro-platform locals took a realistic view of all this, saying with a shrug: 'The Government could have saved a lot of money and a lot of time by building the yard at Drumbuie on the railway line. They would have saved millions. Now they are going to have to carry in everything by sea because Kishorn is supposed to be an "island site".'

Well, it didn't quite work out that way. True that Strome Ferry became important again, as its three acre jetty was infilled with 70,000 tons of stones and rails were laid from the Kyle Line, so that freight brought in could be shuttled by barge over to Kishorn. But heavy traffic was also smashing up the narrow roads and the platform site was growing beyond its boundaries.

This is how a Gaelic-speaking resident of Kishorn put it to me as we stood listening to the thump-thump of pile driving sounding across the water to the village. 'The noise goes on all the time, but we think nothing of it. Better that than nothing, and nothing is what we have had for too long. When you look across the water to the camp at night it's like a battleship with lights. Quite a few local men who had to work away from home have come back. But you have to work a lot of hours to make a good wage.'

As for Kyle of Lochalsh., it is now a multi-million £ supply base for four contractors with platform building yards on the Clyde. From Loch Striven the platforms are towed up to Kyle for the fitting of deck nodules. The Royal Navy are here too, and in Applecross, where a double-width road has been driven up the lonely north coast to Sand which is now a base for testing torpedos in the deepest waters of the Inner Sound.

All this pleases the young, as I discovered when I spoke to some Plockton High School leavers, aged 17, and heard their views. None wanted to leave the Highlands if jobs offering them advancement and worthwhile lives could be found. They were not interested in labouring or tourism, but thought that oil-related developments in the west could be the means of bringing technological training and enabling them to live at home.

There is an important social aspect to this, and it is the geriatric problem, when the able members of a family have to migrate leaving the parents to manage as best they can. The result is that the crofting land goes back, the house falls into disrepair, and there may be loneliness and physical hardship. Work with a future in it will keep alert young people in the district, but there must also be houses for them to live in.

Oil could be a great opportunity for the Western Highlands, provided the social aspect is given a priority over incentives to produce oil from the sea at speed. Ian Noble, Chairman of Seaforth Maritime, speaking with inside knowledge, says: 'The longer our oil remains in the ground, the more valuable it is likely to become'. By going slow we can learn from mistakes inevitable in the new technology of deep water exploration.

It is Gaelic, Norse and Highland culture as much as the environment we have to conserve against an oil industry geared to money. We are in a wartime situation and we badly need wartime controls. The basic priority is to acquire the land, as the Shetlanders realized, but the Government does not—as yet. Next, if we are thinking of a long-term future for the local people, beyond the life of the oil boom in the North Sea, we should be thinking of a total marine-based technology, exploring every aspect of working below the sea, for mineral extraction or fish farming, not to mention research into oil exploration of foreign ocean beds.

The Clyde became famous for ships because it pioneered modern ship-building and engineering. Its products still circulate round the world. The imagination of school-leavers in the north would be stirred if they had technical colleges and a local university to give them the pioneer opportunity here. This is the true way to provide the leaders that Scotland badly needs if we are to seize our place in the world and not be plundered of our resources.

`The West Highlands remain, a beautiful and problem land to live in without the aid of an external income.

Index

Index

Index

Index

Index

Index